The Depth and Richness of the Scriptures

A CATHOLIC APPROACH
TO UNDERSTANDING
THE BIBLE

Dr. Adele J. Gonzalez

get with it.

Cover Design: JMGD, Inc.
Design & Diagramming: Manuel Villaverde

ISBN 0-9761639-3-4

Published by Get-With-It, LLC

Printed by Nu Press of Miami, Inc.
Miami, Florida

DEDICATION

To Zoila, my spiritual sister,
whose unshakable faith
has always been an inspiration for me
and with whom I share
a deep love for the Word of God.

ACKNOWLEDGMENT

I will always be grateful
to the late Father Raymond E. Brown, S.S.,
teacher and model of biblical scholarship.
His lectures and writings nurtured my love
for the Scriptures.

Contents

INTRODUCTION

For the past 32 years, my professional ministry has included teaching the Bible. During this time my own understanding of the Word of God has grown, changed and stretched beyond my wildest expectations. My own process has been a mirror of the process of formation of the Bible itself. As the people's understanding of the revelation of God developed, so did  the writings of the Old and the New Testaments. As the lived experience of the Jewish and Christian communities unfolded, so did their theology and the way they understood God's revelation.

During my years as Parish Director of Religious Education, Formation Director of the School of Ministry of the Archdiocese of Miami, and Adjunct Theology Professor at Barry University, I have developed handouts that have enabled me to pass on to my students the richness and depth of the Scriptures in a way that is user friendly and beneficial to beginners as well as to the more advanced. At the request of many I have compiled my notes in this book so that it can be available to a larger readership.

I thank God for gifting me with a deep love for Scripture, both Old and New Testaments and for the opportunity to teach it. I am also grateful to the many people who have encouraged me with their interest, their questions and their wisdom to continue studying and growing in my understanding of the depth of God's revelation and the awesomeness of God's love.

Adele J. González
January 28, 2005
Revised October 12, 2005

I. Introduction to the "Book"

What is the Bible? Who wrote it?
Who put it together?

- The Bible

The word "Bible" comes from the Greek *ta biblia* which means "the Books." The Bible is a collection of many individual works written over a period of more than 1,000 years. It was written in three different lan-

guages: Hebrew, Aramaic and Greek, and in different places: Palestine, Greece, Babylon, Rome, etc. It contains diverse literary styles which also reflect the personalities and contexts of the authors. Christians believe that despite many authors, the Bible has one author, the Holy Spirit, who inspired the sacred writers.

The sacred authors deeply believed in what they wrote, and the purpose of their writing was to leave a written legacy to present and future believers. Thus, **these books were written by believers for believers.** The Bible is not meant to "prove" the Christian faith to non-believers.

- Inspiration

Christians also believe that **the Bible is inspired**. In general terms, this means that the sacred writers were inspired by God when they wrote the various books. In other words, the

Bible message was originated by the Holy Spirit, but was not "dictated" by God to a single person nor were the events recorded at the exact moment they happened.

> "Those divinely revealed realities which are contained and presented in Sacred Scripture have been committed to writing under the inspiration of the Holy Spirit." (Vatican II Documents: *Dei Verbum* #s 11, 12 & 13)

> "It is important to understand that God in inspiring the sacred writers, took into consideration their personalities, their individual styles, their historical moment, and their cultural backgrounds. All these ideas help the reader understand that the Word of God has been revealed to us through human words.

> "What is the literal sense of a passage is not always as obvious in the speeches and writings of the ancient authors of the East as it is in our own times... The interpreter must go back wholly in spirit to those remote centuries of the East and with the aid of history, archaeology, ethnology and other sciences, accurately determine what modes of writing the authors of that period would be likely to use, and in fact did use." (Pope Pius XII's Encyclical *Divino Afflante Spiritu* on biblical studies, issued in 1943, 35-36)

• Revelation

Christians of all denominations believe that **the Bible contains God's revelation**. It is not considered just a body of truths, but the revelation of God himself who wishes to make known his love for his people.

Are Catholic and Protestant Bibles different?

- The Canon[1] and the Deutero-Canonical Books of the Old Testament

We know that all Bibles are not alike. The New Testament, in both Catholic and Protestant Bibles, are identical. However, there are dissimilarities in the books of the Old Testament. The Catholic Bible contains 46 books in the Old Testament; Protestant and Hebrew Bibles have only 39. What follows is a brief explanation of the causes of this difference.

After the Babylonian Exile in 586 B.C.E. many Jews returned to Palestine, but most stayed in places like Egypt, Syria, Mesopotamia and Greece. These groups were known as "Jews of the *Diaspora*", Greek for dispersion. With the conquests of Alexander the Great, the Greek culture and language became the predominant influence of the known world including the Jewish communities. Around the 3rd Century B.C.E. the Hebrew books were translated into Greek in a work known as the *Septuagint* (**LXX**). The *Septuagint* included seven books originally written in Greek and not used in Palestine by the Hebrew speaking Jews.

In the year 90 C.E. after the destruction of the Temple in Jerusalem, Jewish religious leaders gathered in the city of Jamnia to decide their Canon. They approved the 39 books written in Hebrew or Aramaic and ignored the Greek translation. Meanwhile, the early Christian communities were already familiar with the *Septuagint*, which had wider use in the Greco-Roman world and was more available to Christians

---

[1] Canon comes from the Hebrew word for a reed which was used as a measuring stick. A canon includes the official writings "measured" by a church or religious group and accepted as containing divine revelation.

who, for the most part, were Greek-speaking Gentiles and not Jews. These seven books are called "deutero-canonical" or second canon of inspired books besides those in Hebrew.

Deuterocanonical books:

1 and 2 Maccabees
Judith
Tobit
Baruch
Sirach = Ecclesiasticus = Jesus ben Sira
The Wisdom of Solomon
(Also some passages in the Books of Daniel and Esther)

Protestants often refer to these seven books as the *apocrypha* (hidden books). Catholics apply that term not just to the seven books, but also to works that are not considered inspired by the Christian Canon.

• The New Testament Canon

How was the New Testament compiled?
Why did some writings get included while others did not?
Who made the final decision?

Churches call this the "canonical question." The Catholic Bible contains the 46 books that were first considered canonical by the Synod of Rome under Pope Damasus, in 382 C.E. They were later solemnly approved by the Church during the Council of Trent in April, 1546. This indicates that the books of the NT were selected over an extended period of time and from among a wide variety of Christian literature.

The following criteria was used in identifying a canon of Christian literature:

      a) Apostolicity (apostolic authorship) and antiquity

      b) Historical reliability

      c) Theological correctness

      d) Wide-spread use by the churches

II. THE MEANING OF INSPIRED SCRIPTURE

Is everything in the Bible true?
Can we take every word literally?

• <u>Characteristics of Catholic Interpretation.</u>

(The following notes are taken from the Document, *The Interpretation of the Bible in the Church*. Pontifical Biblical Commission. Libreria Editrice Vaticana. November, 1993. Reprinted in English, *Origins*, VOL.23: NO.29, January 6, 1994).

Catholic exegesis does not claim any particular scientific method as its own. It recognizes that one of the aspects of biblical texts is that they are the work of human authors, who employed both their own capacities for expression and the means which their age and social context put at their disposal. Consequently, Catholic exegesis freely makes use of the scientific method and approaches which allow a better grasp of the meaning of texts in their linguistic, literary, socio-cultural, religious and historical contexts, while explaining them through studying their sources and attending to the personality of each author (*cf. Divino afflante Spiritu, 557*).

The contribution of modern methods of interpretation (*hermeneutics*), has allowed scholars to attribute to every text of Scripture three levels of meaning. While keeping in mind that considerable diversity of opinion prevails, some general principles can be stated:

1. *The Literal Sense.*

It is not only legitimate, it is also absolutely necessary to seek to define the precise meaning of texts as produced by their authors—what is called the "literal" meaning… The literal sense is not to be confused with the "literalist" sense to which fundamentalists are attached. It is not sufficient to translate a text word for word in order to obtain its literal sense. One must understand the text according to the literary conventions of the time. When a text is metaphorical, its literal sense is not that which flows immediately from a word-to-word translation (e.g. "Let your loins be girt": Lk. 12:35), but that which corresponds to the metaphorical use of these terms ("Be ready for action").

The literal sense of Scripture is that which has been expressed directly by the inspired human authors. Since it is the fruit of inspiration, this sense is also intended by God, as principal author. One arrives at this sense by means of a careful analysis of the text, within its literary and historical context. The principal task of exegesis is to carry out this analysis, making use of all the resources of literary and historical research, with a view to defining the literal sense of the biblical texts with the greatest possible accuracy. To this end, the study of ancient literary genres is particularly necessary.

2. *The Spiritual Sense.*

The paschal event, the death and resurrection of Jesus, has established a radically new historical context, which sheds fresh light upon the ancient texts and causes them to undergo a change in meaning. In particular, certain texts which in ancient times had to be thought of as hyperbole (e.g. the oracle where God, speaking of a son of David, promised to establish his throne "forever": 2 Sm. 7:12-13; 1 Chr. 17:11-14), these texts must now be taken literally, because "Christ, having been raised from the dead, dies no more" (Rom. 6:9). Exegetes who... are open to the dynamic aspect of a text will recognize here a profound element of continuity as well as a move to a different level: Christ rules forever, but not on the earthly throne of David (cf also Ps. 2:7-8; 110:1,4)...

As a general rule we can define the spiritual sense, as understood by Christian faith, as the meaning expressed by the biblical texts when read under the influence of the Holy Spirit, in the context of the paschal mystery of Christ and of the new life which flows from it. This context truly exists. In it the New Testament recognizes the fulfillment of the Scriptures. It is therefore quite acceptable to reread the Scriptures in the light of this new context, which is that of life in the Spirit.

3.   *The Fuller Sense.*

The term *fuller sense*, which is relatively recent, has given rise to discussion. The fuller sense is defined as a deeper meaning of the text, intended by God but not clearly expressed by the human author. Its existence in the biblical text comes to be known when one studies the text in the light of other biblical texts which utilize it or in its relationship with the internal development of revelation.

It is then a question either of the meaning that a subsequent biblical author attributes to an earlier biblical text, taking it up in a context which confers upon it a new literal sense, or else it is a question of the meaning that an authentic doctrinal tradition or a conciliar definition gives to a biblical text. For example, the context of Matthew 1:23 gives a fuller sense to the prophecy of Isaiah 7:14.

In a word, one might think of the "fuller sense" as another way of indicating the spiritual sense of a biblical text in the case where the spiritual sense is distinct from the literal sense. It has its foundation in the fact that the Holy Spirit, principal author of the Bible, can guide human authors in the choice of expressions in such a way that the letter will express a truth the fullest depths of which the authors themselves do not perceive.

Why is it so difficult to interpret the Bible? Is it not enough to read it and let the Holy Spirit guide us?

• <u>Hermeneutics (The study of interpretation or the quest for meaning)</u>

(The following notes are taken from the Document, *The Interpretation of the Bible in the Church.* Pontifical Biblical Commission. Libreria Editrice Vaticana. November, 1993. Reprinted in English, *Origins,* VOL.23: NO.29, January 6, 1994).

The problem of the interpretation of the Bible is not new. The Bible itself bears witness that its interpretation can be a difficult matter. *See Acts 8:30-35; 2 Peter 1:20, 3:16.*

<u>The Historical-Critical Method</u> is one of the most widely used methods for the scientific study of the meaning of ancient texts. The Bible, inasmuch as it is the "word of God in human language", has been composed by human authors in all its various parts and in all the sources that lie behind them. Because of this, its proper understanding not only admits the use of this method but actually requires it. At the present stage of its development, the historical-critical method moves through the following steps:

Textual Criticism. The task of Textual Criticism is to establish, according to fixed rules, a biblical text as close as possible to the original. It must compare ancient manuscripts and produce the most authentic reading available. We have none of the originals of the biblical text, only copies of copies. Earliest manuscripts date from c.200 C.E., but most are from the 4th Century and later.

Source Criticism or Literary Criticism. The task of Literary Criticism for a long time came to be identified with the attempt to distinguish in texts different sources. Thus it was that there developed in the 19th century the "documentary hypothesis," which sought to give an explanation of the editing of the Pentateuch. According to this hypothesis, four documents, to some extent parallel with each other, had been woven together: that of the Yahwist (J), that of the Elohist (E), that of the Deuteronomist (D) and that of the Priestly author (P); the final editor made use of this latter (Priestly) document to provide a structure for the whole.

In similar fashion, to explain both the agreements and disagreements between the three synoptic Gospels, scholars had recourse to the "two source" hypothesis. According to this, the Gospels of Matthew and Luke were composed out of two principal sources: on the one hand, the Gospel of Mark and, on the other, a collection of the sayings of Jesus (called Q, from the German word *Quelle*, meaning "source"). In their essential features, these two hypotheses retain their prominence in scientific exegesis today--though they are also under challenge.

Genre Criticism seeks to identify literary genres, the social milieu that gave rise to them, their particular features and the history of their development. *Form Criticism* tries to discover the oral tradition behind the written text; to discover the "setting in life" in which these traditions arose. Form criticism as a method of literary study of the Gospels seeks to sort out the stories about Jesus and classify them according to their oral forms. It also seeks to reconstruct the previous history of a story as an oral tradition before it was fixed as part of a written Gospel narrative.

Tradition Criticism situates texts in the stream of tradition and attempts to describe the development of this tradition over the course of time. Finally, *Redaction Criticism* studies the modifications that these texts have undergone before being fixed in their final state, it also analyzes this final stage, trying as far as possible to identify the tendencies particularly characteristic of this concluding process.

When this last method was brought into play, the whole series of different stages characteristic of the historical-critical method became complete: From *textual criticism* one progresses to *literary criticism*, with its work of dissection in the *quest for sources*; then one moves to a *critical study of forms* and, finally, to an analysis of the *editorial process*, which aims to be particularly attentive to the text as it has been put together. All this has made it possible to understand far more accurately the intention of the authors and editors of the Bible as well as the message which they addressed to their first readers. The achievement of these results has lent the historical-critical method an importance of the highest order.

Yet, no scientific method for the study of the Bible is fully adequate to comprehend the biblical texts in all their richness. For all its overall validity, the historical-critical method cannot claim to be totally sufficient in this respect. It necessarily has to leave aside many aspects of the writings which it studies. It is not surprising, then, that at the present time other methods and approaches are proposed which serve to explore more profoundly other aspects worthy of attention.

Why do some people get almost violent
when they quote the Bible to support their ideas?

• Fundamentalist Interpretation

"Fundamentalist interpretation starts from the principle that the Bible, being the word of God, inspired and free from error, should be read and interpreted literally in all its details. But by "literal interpretation" it understands a naively literalist interpretation, one, that is to say, which excludes every effort at understanding the Bible that takes account of its historical origins and development. It is opposed, therefore, to the use of the historical-critical method, as indeed to the use of any other scientific method for the interpretation of Scripture... It demands... a reading of the Bible which rejects all questioning and any kind of critical research.

"The basic problem with fundamentalist interpretation of this kind is that, refusing to take into account the historical character of biblical revelation, it makes itself incapable of accepting the full truth of the incarnation itself. As regards relationships with God, fundamentalism seeks to escape any closeness of the divine and the human. It refuses to admit that the inspired word of God has been expressed in human language and that this word has been expressed, under divine inspiration, by human authors possessed of limited capacities and resources. For this reason, it tends to treat the biblical text as if it had been dictated word for word by the Spirit. It fails to recognize that the word of God has been formulated in language and expression conditioned by various periods. It pays no attention to the literary forms and to the human ways of thinking to be found in the biblical texts, many of which are the result of a process extending over long periods of time and bearing the mark of very diverse historical situations.

"Fundamentalism also places undue stress upon the inerrancy of certain details in the biblical texts, especially in what concerns historical events or supposedly scientific truth. It often historicizes material which from the start never claimed to be historical. It considers historical everything that is reported or recounted with verbs in the past tense, failing to take the necessary account of the possibility of symbolic or figurative meaning.

"In what concerns the Gospels, fundamentalism does not take into account the development of the Gospel tradition, but naively confuses the final stage of this tradition (what the evangelists have written) with the initial (the words and deeds of the historical Jesus). At the same time fundamentalism neglects an important fact: The way in which the first Christian communities themselves understood the impact produced by Jesus of Nazareth and his message. But it is precisely there that we find a witness to the apostolic origin of the Christian faith and its direct expression. Fundamentalism thus misrepresents the call voiced by the Gospel itself.

"Fundamentalism likewise tends to adopt very narrow points of view. It accepts the literal reality of an ancient, out-of-date cosmology simply because it is found expressed in the Bible; this blocks any dialogue with a broader way of seeing the relationship between culture and faith. Its relying upon a non-critical reading of certain texts of the Bible serves to reinforce political ideas and social attitudes that are marked by prejudices--racism, for example--quite contrary to the Christian Gospel.

"Finally... it fails to realize that the New Testament took form within the Christian church and that it is the Holy Scripture of this church, the existence of which preceded the composition of the texts. Because of this, fundamentalism is often anti-church, it considers of little importance the creeds, the doctrines and liturgical practices which have become part of church tradition, as well as the teaching function of the church itself. It presents itself as a form of private interpretation which does not acknowledge that the church is founded on the Bible and draws its life and inspiration from Scripture.

"The fundamentalist approach is dangerous, for it is attractive to people who look to the Bible for ready answers to the problems of life. It can deceive these people, offering them interpretations that are pious but illusory, instead of telling them that the Bible does not necessarily contain an immediate answer to each and every problem. Without saying as much in so many words, fundamentalism actually invites people to a kind of intellectual suicide. It injects into life a false certitude, for it unwittingly confuses the divine substance of the biblical message with what are in fact its human limitations.

"It is important for every Catholic to realize that the church produced the New Testament, not vice versa. The Bible did not come down from heaven, whole and intact, given by the Holy Spirit. Just as the experience and faith of Israel developed its sacred books, so was the early Christian Church the matrix of the New Testament. The Catholic Church has authoritatively told us which books are inspired by the Holy Spirit and therefore canonical.

"The Bible, then, is the church's book. The New Testament did not come before the church, but from the church. Peter and the other Apostles were given special authority to teach and govern before the New Testament was written. The first generation of Christians had no New Testament at all -- but they were the church then, just as we are the church today."

(*Pastoral Statement for Catholics on Biblical Fundamentalism*, National Conference of Catholic Bishops Ad Hoc Committee on Biblical Fundamentalism, March 26, 1987)

Can you give me some examples of biblical fundamentalism?

The fundamentalist view of the Bible can be found among Christians of all denominations. Fundamentalism is not a doctrine, but a way of looking and understanding life and events. A fundamentalist person can miss the "fundamental" message of Scripture.

Examples:

✦ **The Beatitudes:**

    ↗ *The Sermon on the Mount?* (Matthew 5:1ff.)
    ↘ *The Sermon on the Plain?* (Luke 6:17ff.)

What is the fundamental message in these readings? The mountain? The plain? Going up or coming down? The disciples or the multitudes following Jesus? The power coming from him? His compassion for the suffering and afflicted? The healing? The beatitudes?

✦ **Jesus' first miracle:**

← *A synagogue in Capernaum, a man with an unclean spirit?* (Mark 1:23-26)
→ *The wedding in Cana of Galilee, turning water into wine?* (John 2:1-11)

Which was the first one? Is one of them untrue? What is their importance?

✦ *The Sabbath:*

▲ "Then God spoke all these words: I am the Lord your God, who brought you out of the land of Egypt... Remember the Sabbath day, and keep it holy. Six days you shall labor and do all your work. But the seventh day is a Sabbath to the Lord your God; you shall not do any work..." (Exodus 20:2,8-10)

▲ "Again he entered the synagogue, and a man was there with a withered hand. They watched him to see if he would cure him on the Sabbath, so that they might accuse him..." (Mark 3:1ff.)

▲ "Now he was teaching in one of the synagogues on the Sabbath. And just then there appeared a woman with a spirit that had crippled her for eighteen years. She was bent over..." (Luke 13:10ff.)

▲ "At that time Jesus went through the grain fields on the Sabbath; his disciples were hungry and they began to pluck heads of grain and to eat.... For the Son of Man is Lord of the Sabbath." (Matthew 12:1-8)

What should we believe about the Sabbath? Did Jesus break the Law?

✦   *On the Law:*

✄ "Do not think that I have come to abolish the law or the prophets... Whoever breaks one of the least of these commandments, and teaches others to do the same, will be called least in the kingdom of heaven..." (Matthew 5:17-19)

◢ "You have heard that it was said, 'an eye for and eye and a tooth for a tooth.'

◣ "But I say to you, Do not resist an evildoer. But if anyone strike you on the right cheek..."   (Matthew 5:38-39)

◢ "You have heard that it was said, 'You shall love your neighbor and hate your enemy.'

◣ "But I say to you, Love your enemies and pray for those who persecute you." (Matthew 5:43-44)

Obey or change? What do you think Jesus did?

III. THE OLD TESTAMENT (HEBREW SCRIPTURES)

What is the Old Testament or Hebrew Bible?

- The Hebrew Bible (Old Testament) is also called *TaNaK.*

  ■ The books of the Hebrew Bible are grouped into three categories:

    - Torah (Law, instruction) – 5 books
    - Nebiim (Prophets) – 21 books
    - Ketubim (Writings) – 13 books

    They have:

    - One central theme:
      The **Covenant** with the One God
    - Two central events:
      Exodus — c.1250 B.C.E.
      Babylonian Exile — 587 B.C.E.
    - Three central figures:
      Abraham   Moses   David

- The Catholic Bible divides the Old Testament books into four categories (same books as in the Hebrew Bible, but different divisions):

  - Pentateuch (The Law)
  - Historical Books
  - Wisdom Writings
  - Prophetic Literature

- There are 7 additional books in the Catholic Old Testament that do not appear in the Jewish canon. *(See pg. 6)*

What is the significance of the "Covenant" in the Old Testament?

- <u>The Covenant</u>

The relationship between *Yahweh* and Israel is better understood in terms of Covenant, a free agreement which has YHWH as its author. **YHWH invites Israel to be His People (the People of God)**, and Israel answers primarily in the Exodus-Sinai experience under the leadership of Moses. *(See Ex 19-24 and 33)*

Before the Exodus experience, the theme of the Covenant was already present in the relationship between God and Abraham (Gen 15), renewed with Isaac (Gen 26), and renewed yet again with Jacob (Gen 28). It was also implicit in the stories of Creation and the Flood. Yet it was not until Ex 3 and 24 that we find the Covenant finally sealed with Moses and the people on Sinai.

In the Old Testament we find a series of blessings and promises that lead up to fulfillment at Sinai. These include:

- Gen 1:25-26   God blesses Creation with Adam and Eve
- Gen 9:1-7   God renews the blessing with Noah
- Gen 17   God gives further promise to Abraham
- Ex 6   God prepares a new covenant with Moses

All of biblical history may be called a theology of the Covenant. The concept was at the heart of Israel's religious beliefs:

- They are bound to an unbreakable covenant-union with their God
- God has made known his love and mercy to them
- God has given them commandments to guide their daily life
- They owe God worship, fidelity and obedience
- They are marked by the sign of the covenant-bond

Israel is "formed" as a people by means of the Covenant. Israel, the nation, was a Theocracy [YHWH was the ruler].

YHWH pledges Himself to the Covenant in terms of:

     loving kindness/mercy   [

                               ] steadfast covenant love

     fidelity   [

What was expected of the people in return?

• <u>The response to the Covenant agreement</u>

YHWH demands the same two qualities (fidelity and mercy) from Israel and the Israelites, both in terms of their relationship with YHWH and with each other. When Israel becomes unfaithful to the Covenant, YHWH reminds her about it, through prophets, exile, and catastrophes.

Israel is to be faithful to the Covenant both spiritually and existentially:

(1) Keeping the Torah/Law, which is an expression of the spiritual covenant;

(2) Living in loving kindness, by caring for the *anawin*, the poor of Yahweh (orphans, widows and the aliens), and by being just in all dealings with fellow Israelites.

<u>Example</u>

Micah 6:8: Yahweh does not want material sacrifices at all, but a quality of inner commitment:

> *justice* = right relationships with one's brothers-and-sisters-in-community
> *kindness* = a compassionate faithfulness toward others-in-community
> *a humble walk with God* = the loving commitment of all that one is to God

Justice in ancient Israel was a term used to describe the wholesome relations which exist within a community when the rights of individuals are honored and preserved.

Kindness implied more than simple benevolence. It is a relational term and it means something like "faithfulness to others within the community." The Hebrew word is often used to describe God's covenant faithfulness to Israel.

Walk humbly with your God. The Hebrew word translated "humbly" is rare in the Old Testament, occurring only here and (in a different form) in Proverbs 11:2 where it is contrasted with "pride." Seen in this light, humble does not mean some quality of passivity or self-abasement (as the English word sometimes implies), but rather the ability to view oneself in a proper relation to God, that is, to be aware of one's need of, and openly to acknowledge one's dependence upon God.

God wants not what we have but who we are, ourselves and nothing else. It is not surprising that the prophets often provoked the anger of those who felt that God could be bought off or manipulated.

(Some notes are taken from *The Hebrew Prophets*, by James D. Newsome, Jr. Atlanta: John Knox Press, 1984, and *Reading the Old Testament*, by Lawrence Boadt, New York: Paulist Press, 1984.)

What is the meaning of the word YHWH? Where did it originate?

• The Name of God: YAHWEH *(See Exodus 3:10-14)*

At the burning bush, God revealed to Moses his plan to save Israel, and also his own Name. A confused Moses asked God: *"When the Israelites ask me, 'What is his Name?' what shall I answer them?"* and God said to Moses, *"I am who I am; and thus you will say to the Israelites, I am has sent me to you."*

Interpretations:

1. "I AM WHO I AM" - Some scholars understand the verb "to be" as expressing absolute being. Yahweh would then mean, "He who is", or "He who causes what is," in contrast to all other beings, which do not exist of themselves, and in opposition to the gods of the nations, which are nothing.

2. For the ancient Semites, the knowledge of a name brought with it power over the things or persons named. To know the name of a god meant to have the power of invoking the god efficaciously with the certainty of being heard. Some interpret that the true God does not place godself at the mercy of humans by revealing the name that expresses His essence. These authors think that "Yahweh" is not a name, but the term given by God by which people are to address Him.

3. God's answer may be in reality a refusal to answer, and at the same time an assertion of God's mysterious otherness, the God who is beyond naming and therefore beyond human's power to control. God will not be known by a name, but by what He does. Thus, for generations to come, the mysterious designation of God, YAHWEH, would always be associated with God's saving deed: the Exodus.

4. After the Exile, for motives of reverence based upon Exodus 20:7, and Leviticus 24:16, the Jews ceased to pronounce the letters YHWH. When it occurred, they read *Adonai*, Lord. Later, the Massorites (group of Jewish scholars of the 8th to 11th centuries C.E.), attached the vowels of this word to the consonants of the unpronounceable Name. This gave rise to the medieval *Jehovah*, a word that has no meaning, and the

true pronunciation was lost. Today, scholars are fairly well agreed that the original form was *Yahweh*.

5. The *Septuagint* (Greek translation of the O.T., c.3rd Century B.C.E. used by the Jews outside of Palestine), translated YAHWEH as **KYRIOS**, Lord.

6. The *Vulgate* (Latin translation of the Christian Bible by St. Jerome in the fifth century C.E.) used the Latin **DOMINUS**.

What is the Pentateuch? Did Moses write it?

• The Pentateuch

The Name Pentateuch means a five-part writing, that is, one book in five volumes. They are the foundation documents for the people of Israel and Jewish tradition calls it *Torah*, which is often translated as "Law", but really means "teaching" or "instruction." These books are:

▪ *Genesis.-* Opens up with the "history" of Creation and takes us to Joseph and the anticipation of God's great act of deliverance from Egypt.

▪ *Exodus.-* Tells the story of how God chose Moses to deliver Israel from slavery in Egypt and led them to enter into the covenant relationship.

▪ *Leviticus.-* Contains the laws and commandments that God gave to his people. These regulations dealt mostly with sacrifice, feasts, ritual obligations, etc.

▪ *Numbers.-* Adds more laws and regulations about the twelve tribes and their organization. Chapters 10-20 continue the story of Israel's journey in the desert, complete with a 40 year punishment for her constant rebellion against God and Moses.

■   *Deuteronomy* (or a second Law" in Greek).- A later book composed as a reflective speech of Moses. It is Moses' "farewell speech" and supposedly takes place just as the people are ready to invade the Promised Land.

For more than 2,000 years Moses was considered the author of the Pentateuch which was called "the Book of Moses." But even in the ancient world some questioned whether Moses could really have written the entire Pentateuch including his own death in Deuteronomy 34:5-12!

Most scholars agree that the Pentateuch did not exist in its present state until approximately 450 B.C.E., nearly 800 years after Moses' death. Although no one can say for certain who wrote the Pentateuch, there is no question that it summarizes and reflects the teachings and the traditions given by God to Moses and handed down orally for centuries. Moses played a central and unique role in the events recorded in these books and is regarded as the founder of the Israelite faith.

If Moses himself did not write the Pentateuch, who put it together?

• Four sources theory
(Adapted from the *Collegeville Bible Commentary #3, the New Jerome Biblical Commentary and the Catholic Bible (NAB)*, Personal Study Edition)

Scholars noticed that there were two different Hebrew names given to the Deity in the Book of Genesis: Yahweh, the personal Name of Israel's God, and Elohim, translated simply God. The presence of these different names in various stories coincided with differences in style and vocabulary in the stories in which they appeared. Contradictions within stories (for example, Gen 6:19 and 7:2), where resolved when these stories were divided, on the basis of the use of the Divine Name, into what were originally two independent traditions or sources.

By the mid-1800s and after careful analysis of the data, scholars concluded that there were at least four different authors/sources who contributed to the formation of the Pentateuch. Eventually, a German scholar, Julius Wellhausen, proposed dates for the writing of each version and speculated on the historical context that required different ways of telling the history:

- Yahwist (J, for German Jahvist) - Written in Jerusalem in the 10th or 9th Century B.C.E. to show that promises to Abraham were fulfilled in the kingdom of David. Uses the name *Yahweh* for God.

- Elohist (E) - Written after the split of the kingdom after 900 B.C.E. to provide the Northern kingdom's official account of the tradition. Uses the name *Elohim* for God.

- Priestly (P) - Much of the material dates to the 8th and 7th Centuries B.C.E., but some were probably written in the 6th Century B.C.E. It reflects and responds to the needs of the exiles in the 6th Century. God is more distant and less intimately involved with humans. "P" is the dominant tradition in Pentateuch and reflects the Southern kingdom's point of view.

  The P editors arranged the four sources into our present Pentateuch around 500 B.C.E.

- Deuteronomic (D) - The Book of Deuteronomy was considered a fourth and totally separate source, and received the label "D". - Written in the 8th and 7th Centuries B.C.E. It reassesses the J and E traditions in light of pagan influence and unfaithful kings.

IV. BRIEF HISTORY OF ISRAEL
IN ANCIENT TIMES

Were the books written while the events occurred?
Was God "dictating" or were the sacred authors relating
what God was inspiring them to write?

• A relational God

According to the Old Testament, God revealed himself through historical events. God liberated, established a Covenant, guided and protected the people. God was actively involved in the lives of the Israelites. Thus, the Old Testament is a reflection and a religious interpretation of the history of the people of Israel.

Chronology of the Old Testament

All dates are B.C.E. (Before the Common Era), and were taken from John Bright's, *A History of Israel*. Philadelphia: Westminster Press, 1981.

(See pages 32 & 33)

Date	Writings	Events and books that describe them
?	-------	Pre-history: Creation and Fall *(Genesis)*
c.1850-1750	-------	The Patriarchs: Abraham, Isaac, Jacob/Israel Jacob's clan goes to Egypt *(Genesis)*
c. 1280?	--------	The Exodus from Egypt: Moses, the Sinai Covenant, *the Torah* *(Exodus, Leviticus, Numbers, Deuteronomy)*
c.1250 - 1200	-------	The Conquest of Palestine *(Joshua)*
c.1200 - 1020	-------	Judges. Charismatic leaders: Samson, Deborah, Gideon, and **Samuel***(considered the last of the judges* *and the first of the prophets)* *(Judges)*
c.1020 - 922	**c.950 (J)** **Tradition**	The Kingdom united: Saul (1020), David (1000), Solomon (961). Samuel, Nathan, Elijah, Elisha (non-writing prophets) *(1 & 2 Samuel, 1 & 2 Kings, 1 & 2 Chronicles)*
c. 922	**Prophets** **c.750 (E)** **c.700 (J+E)**	The Kingdom split into two: north and south ▶ Northern Israel (922 to 722/1). Fall of Samaria. Exile in Asiria. Begins the time of the classical prophets with Amos and Hosea ▶ Judah to the south (922 to 587). Fall of Jerusalem and destruction of the Temple. Babilonian Exile. The great prophets *Isaiah, Jeremiah, and Ezekiel.*

Date	Writings	Events and books that describe them
	c.550 (D); (JE+D) & (P)	
538	"	The Persians under King Cyrus capture Babylon and free the Israelites.
520	"	The Temple in Jerusalem is rebuilt. Post-exilic life of Israel under Nehemiah and Ezra. *(Nehemiah, Ezra, 1 & 2 Chronicles)*
	c.500+ JED+P = Pentateuch **Wisdom tradition** *[Proverbs, Job, Ecclesiastes]*	
c.398		Palestine under Persian domination
c.336-323		Greek invasion under Alexander the Great
200		Translation of the Hebrew Scriptures (OT) into Greek: *The Septuagint* **(LXX)**
167		The Greeks persecute the Jewish faith
164		The struggle for religious freedom under Mattathias. *(1 & 2 Maccabees, Daniel)*
63		POMPEY conquers PALESTINE (Roman control)
37		HEROD the Great rules the Jews in Judea
6?		**BIRTH OF JESUS**

If nothing was written before the 10th Century B.C.E.,
how can we interpret the stories that tell
of events that happened
thousands of years before they were "recorded?"

Note: Review the definition of Inspiration on pages 3 and 4.

• The Book of Genesis

Genesis is concerned with origins - of the world, of human beings, of Israel and its ancestors. It covers a vast amount of time, stretching from the beginning of the world down to about 1500 B.C.E.

According to geologists, the earth is at least four billion years old, and some anthropologists believe that we humans have been around at least two million of those years. The authors of Genesis did not know much about this long history, nor did they care. They wished to sketch instead a few highlights about human origins that had particular religious significance for Israel's view of life, and to record a few traditions about their own ancestors that would help them understand how they came to be a people and a nation.

- The title Genesis comes from the word 'generation' and the final editor of the book, the "P" author, in the 6th Century B.C.E. during the Babylonian Exile, organized his material into large blocks introduced by the words "these are the generations of..." The formula occurs ten times in Genesis and serves as a general guide through the stories.

- The Book is the story of the pre-history of Israel. Israel became a nation only when it came to occupy and rule the land of Canaan. This nation came to identify itself as a federation of tribes in covenant with a God who had brought their ancestors out of Egypt and led them to the Promised Land.

■ The Exodus was interpreted as the moment of birth for this nation *(1300-1250 B.C.E.)*.

■ As time passed, they began to realize that even before the time of Exodus, God was at work leading them to that moment. The Exodus was seen as the culmination of the process that started when God first called Abraham and promised to make him a great nation.

■ Eventually, Israel began to view its own history in the context of world history, and joined to the story of its origins the story of the beginnings of the universe and the history of humanity in the primeval period. This process took centuries. Stories were told and retold, adapted and reinterpreted. The Book of Genesis bears the mark of this long process.

• Composition

Scholars divide it in two parts: Chapters 1-11 and 12-50. The first eleven chapters, known as the "primeval history," discuss the Creation of the world and the first human beings—the ancestors of all humanity. It is set in a time before human history. Genesis 1-11 falls into the literary category of "myth."[2] The second part, describes the specific ancestors of Israel itself.

---

2 *"Myth" has different meanings. When biblical scholars use the term they do not refer to something that is false or unreliable, but to an attempt by ancient peoples to explain how certain things came into existence through the action of God. Myth narrates a "sacred history" and is therefore a sacred story.

Does this mean that nothing in Genesis is true?

In Mesopotamian culture, the model for most accounts in Genesis 1-11, scribes explored beginnings through stories, not through abstract or scientific reasoning. The biblical writers produced a version of the common Mesopotamian story of the origins of the populated world, exploring major questions about God and humanity through story.

We must remember that more than being a book *of* or *by* God, the Bible is a book *about* God. Through its many stories, the Pentateuch reveals a God Israel has come to know as the one God, who acts in human history, and who has chosen Israel in a special way. Genesis is not a book of science or of history as we understand it today, rather it is a book of faith written by believers for believers. Yet, it is not a random collection of colorful episodes, but a consciously planned narrative inspired by God to convey a message to the readers. Regardless of the literary categories used in Genesis, scholars agree on what it reveals about the origins of humanity:

- O God is good and all God created is good and beautiful.
- O Human beings are created in the image and likeness of God.
- O Creation is not the result of an accident. God is the primary actor, and Creation is the result of God's action.
- O God has blessed human life.
- O Filled with pride, human beings sin and disobey God.
- O The origin of darkness, which symbolized evil and terror in the ancient world, is left in mystery.
- O God is a God of mercy and justice and loves the human race.

○   Abraham is chosen to bring God's blessing to all.

(Sources: Collegeville Bible Commentary #2, Collegeville: The Liturgical Press, 1985. Lawrence Boadt, *Reading the Old Testament*, New York: Paulist Press, 1984. *The New Jerome Bible Handbook*, Collegeville: The Liturgical Press, 1993).

• Genesis 12-50: The Patriarchs

Part two of Genesis focuses on the history of one family that lived in Northern Mesopotamia and portrays them as the heroic ancestors of the Jewish people, the Patriarchs. There are twelve chapters on Abraham, two on Isaac, nine on Jacob, and ten on Joseph. The lifetimes of the Patriarchs are clearly set before the period in which Israel was in Egypt, and so can be dated no later than the 14th century B.C.E.

▪   The story of Abraham: his call and response; his blessing and promise. (*Gen 12-25*)
▪   The stories of Abraham's son Isaac and grandson Jacob and how they carry on the blessing. (*Gen 26-36*)
▪   The story of Joseph in Egypt: preparation for God's great self-revelation in the Exodus event. (*Gen 37-50*)

Most scholars agree that the customs and events described in these chapters best fit the period from 1900 to 1500 B.C.E. For example, the story of Joseph rising to the position of prime minister in Egypt reflects the period of history around 1500.

• The Book of Exodus

Most authorities place the Exodus in the 13th century B.C.E. According to these authorities the Pharaoh who oppressed the Israelites was Ramses II, the great builder of the New Kingdom who reigned from 1290 to 1224 B.C.E.

The Exodus or the going out from Egypt lies at the very heart of Israel's faith experience. It marks the real beginning of the history of Israel as a people. Before Exodus, the traditions spoke of clans and persons. Now every text speaks of a nation unified by faithfulness to a God who has chosen them for a special role. The God who acted on Israel's behalf was not an insignificant deity of the ancient Near East cut off from reality and relegated to the realm of mythical time. Rather, Israel's God dramatically entered the arena of real time and real people. The variety of literary types in this popular literature witnesses to the variety of human efforts to capture a central experience.

Given the centrality of the Exodus for Israel's faith, it is not surprising to find a number of theologians at work. Exegetes usually point to at least three theologians in the composition of this work:

■ The first is the Yahwist (J): God walks and talks with people. It stresses the blessing.
■ The second is the Elohist (E): God is Elohim and speaks in dreams, etc. It stresses the fear of the Lord.
■ The third is the Priestly Writer (P): who struggles to offer a picture of hope during the debacle of the Exile in the Sixth Century B.C.E. God is Elohim and it presents a cultic approach to God. It stresses the need to obey the Law. As we said before, P is considered the redactor since P is the final teller of the tale.

(Adapted from *The Collegeville Bible Commentary #3*, The New Jerome Biblical Commentary, and Lawrence Boadt's *Reading the Old Testament*, Paulist Press, 1984.)

• The Jewish Feast of the Passover

Each year Jews all over the world gather to celebrate the time when a group of Hebrew slaves in ancient Egypt escaped from their bondage and left behind the land of their captivity. The Jewish celebration that has for centuries commemorated this event is known as Passover. The Seder meal is a combination of banquet, religious service and study session to commemorate the Passover.

Why is this important for Catholics?

This feast has special significance for Catholics because according to the Synoptic Gospels (Matthew, Mark and Luke) it was in the context of the Seder Meal of the Passover feast that Jesus celebrated what has come to be known as the Lord's Supper. When Catholics gather to celebrate the Eucharist they are celebrating a liturgical act that has its roots in the Jewish Passover ritual. These are excerpts of the readings:

-"Why is this night different from all other nights?"
-"Tonight is different from all the other nights because, by this Seder Service, we recall our deliverance from Egypt and from the House of Bondage, as we read:

> 'We were slaves unto Pharaoh in Egypt and the Lord our God brought us forth with a mighty hand and an outstretched arm. It is, therefore, our duty from year to year to celebrate this event and to tell the story of the Exodus over and over again. Indeed to dwell at length on it is a real *Mitzvah* (joy). For the more we talk about it, the better we will understand what a terrible thing slavery is and we shall then try harder to help achieve freedom for ourselves, for our people and for people everywhere.'"

"Retelling the story of the Exodus serves a holy purpose: to take the ancient central, sacred story of redemption from oppression and make it live in a new way in the lives of the contemporary community. 'In every generation, each one of us must feel as if we ourselves have gone forth from Egypt.'

"Passover reminds Jews and *all spiritual seekers* that, if we look closely enough, we may each be able to see our own life stories of liberation and redemption unfolding in the dusty, wine-stained pages of an ancient tale."

(Notes taken from *The Secret Message of the Seder: Passover Past and Future,* by Rabbi Michael L. Feshbach, aol transmitted: 3/19/96; and *From Redemption to Redeemers: The Meaning of Passover,* also by Rabbi Feshbach)

V. Life in the Promised Land

What happened after the Exodus experience?

• <u>The Historical Books</u>
(Notes taken from Lawrence Boadt's *Reading the Old Testament*)

The Book of Joshua opens the section of the Scriptures called the Historical Books. They include all the books that the Jews call the Former Prophets. They were originally edited as a single continuous history of Israel from the days of Moses down to the Babylonian exile.

Joshua -   Chapters 2-12 describe the miraculous conquest of the land by the tribes under Joshua's leadership.
Chapters 13-22 tell how Joshua divided the land among the tribes and settled all the boundary and territorial disputes.

Judges -   Continues the story of Israel's conquest and gradual occupation of the whole land. It tells the stories and legends of Israel's time of tribal life in Palestine which lasted about two hundred years, from 1250 down to a little after 1050 B.C.E.

**The Books of 1 and 2 Samuel,
and 1 and 2 Kings**

Trace the last days of the period of the judges and the first days of Israel as a monarchy.

The difference of theme between the books of Samuel and the books of Kings is that in Samuel, the institution of the monarchy in Israel and the legitimacy of the Davidic dynasty takes prominence, while in Kings, the stress is on the infidelity of the kings of Israel to the Covenant, an infidelity that was, according to the author, the cause of the destruction of both the northern and the southern kingdoms.

What can we learn from the election, anointing, significance and sinfulness of all the kings of Israel?

• <u>The transition in Israel from theocracy to monarchy</u>

Five significant figures in these books are:

▪ **Samuel,** priest and seer; the last of the judges and the first of the prophets
(1 Sam 7:2-17). The people asked him for a king like that of the other nations.
Establishment of the Monarchy (1 Sam 8:1 - 12:25)

▪ **Saul,** first king of Israel (1 Sam 13:1 - 15:35)

- **David**, young aide of Saul's and next king (1 Sam
  16:1 - 2 Sam 5:6 - 24:25)

  - □ **Nathan,** prophet who confronted David:
    "You are that man" (2 Sam 12:7), even
    though David paid his salary!

- **Solomon,** both the most successful king Israel ever
  had, and the one who turned away from YHWH's
  commands into a practical idolatry.
  (1 Kgs 1:1 - 11:43)

- The Kingdom split into two

When Solomon died after a forty year reign, the kingdom
became divided. This period of divided monarchy lasted
from 930 to 586 B.C.E. The kingdom of the North called itself
Israel, and the kingdom of the South, Judah, because it was
still loyal to the house of David and Solomon. It was made
up of only the tribe of Judah. (1 Kgs 12:2 - 2 Kgs 17:41)

- The importance of the Land for Israel

Israel always understood the land to be a gift from Yahweh.
Before the conquest of Canaan, the Patriarchs in Genesis were
portrayed as landless. The land is a gift of Yahweh, but it will
also be a source of temptation to forget Yahweh and follow
Baal and other pagan deities when the people prosper there.
It is the land of the Covenant, so its possession and obedience to Covenant's Law go hand in hand.

Note: Other historical books are: 1 & 2 Chronicles, Ezra, Nehemiah,
Ruth, Esther and Lamentations. *Judith, Tobit, Baruch and 1 & 2
Maccabees* were originally written in Greek and included only in
the Greek *Septuagint*. Today they are only accepted as canonical by
Catholics. *(See page 6).*

Who were the prophets? Could they predict the future?

- The prophetic movement in Israel

The word prophet in the biblical tradition comes from the Greek *profeta*

PRO TO SPEAK	predicting or simply confronting
BEFORE	in front of the people

A biblical prophet was a person deeply concerned with the events that threatened the Covenant relationship between Yahweh and the people of Israel. They did not predict the future; rather, taking on the perspective of God the prophet was concerned about justice, especially towards the poor, the afflicted, aliens, orphans and widows. Prophets took on the mind of God and made it their own so that they dared speak for God, often using the phrase, "Thus says the Lord..."

In speaking from the perspective of God, the prophets always denounced the injustices and pointed out and accused the wrongdoers, hoping for repentance and reform.

The prophetic experiences of God, while conditioned by the worldview of those who underwent them, were deeply rooted in the conviction that God had a will for the world, and especially for the people of Israel, and in the conviction that God was concerned enough about the human race to communicate that will.

Example: Isaiah 6. The prophet's total being was overwhelmed by the presence of God. **The most important part of the experience was the word which God was summoning the prophet to speak.** The danger of **magic** was always present (1 Sam 28:3). True prophecy was to be distinguished not by the quality of the ecstasy which accompanied it but by the content of the oracle. The main concern of the Hebrew prophets was not how they received a word from God, but what that word was.

■ The development and rise of the prophetic movement in Israel was due to three major factors:

1) **The degeneracy of *Yahwism* because of *religious Syncretism.***
The influence of the worship of Baal (Canaanite religion) was very deep and it was the constant preoccupation of the prophets. Depending upon the time and the leader, the king, the influence of the Canaanite religion was felt to varying degrees. This constant battle affected the religion of Yahwism. The syncretistic practices caused the prophets to rise up against this influence and to cry out against their infidelity to Yahweh.

2) **The change from a theocracy to a monarchy.**
Israel rejected the guiding hand of Yahweh and became a politically autonomous entity. The people cried out for a king like the other nations.

3) **The economic and social developments of both Judah and Israel.**
The 12 tribe system had been replaced by a state with a king. Is it naïve to ask if the "people of God" were still the "people of God?"

- <u>Pre-canonical prophets</u>

Three prophetic figures helped to shape the course of prophecy into the classical period:

> • Nathan: literal Hebrew "he gave." Court prophet to King David. Important appearances: 2 Sam 7:1-17; 12:1-13 (**12:7!**); 1 Kgs 1:5-53. Nathan appears as a court prophet of unusual courage and skill, and helps to create a model which many of the later "canonical" prophets are to use.

> • Elijah: literally "Yahweh is God." His story is told in 1 Kgs 17 to 2 Kgs 2.
> Incidents of special interest: 1 Kgs 18:20-40; 19 & 21. In the late prophetic tradition, his return was expected before the final outpouring of God's judgment (Mal 4:5). And among the earliest Christians he was identified with John the Baptist (Jn 1:21) and even with Jesus (Mt 16:14).

> • Elisha: literally "God is Salvation." Follower and successor of Elijah. His stories are filled with miraculous elements that make it hard to portray the kind of spiritual and moral zeal which characterized Elijah. See 2 Kgs 2:23-25 and 6:1-7.

- <u>Unwritten prophets</u>

Although considered prophets, Nathan and Samuel had no books attributed to them. It is important to keep in mind the difference between the prophets and the books attributed to them.

- Writing Prophets

Major	*Minor*	
Isaiah	Hosea	Joel
Jeremiah	Amos	Obadiah
Ezekiel	Jonah	Micah
(Daniel)*	Nahum	Haggai
	Habakkuk	Zechariah
	Zephaniah	Malachi

* In Hebrew, Daniel is not a prophet. Jews consider the Book of Daniel part of the Writings. Christians keep it under Prophets as part of their tradition, but it must be seen as part of the Writings.

Old Testament prophecy is unique in that nowhere outside Israel were there to be spokespersons for God of the stature of Amos, Jeremiah, and the second Isaiah.

- Some examples of prophets

Amos: prophet of God's justice
The first of the Canonical Prophets

A shepherd from the region of the village of Tekoa, a few miles south of Jerusalem. He traveled to the Northern religious center of Bethel, the most important shrine of Yahweh worship in the Northern Kingdom at that time.

Date of Amos' work: c.760 B.C.E.

Location:
The Northern Centers of Bethel and Samaria (the capital of the Northern Kingdom). While the prophet was a southerner (1:1), his work was done in the Northern Kingdom (7:10).

Amos began a new era in the history of Hebrew prophecy. For the first time the words of a prophetic individual were preserved and gathered together.

What led to this new literary style?

• Amos's preaching demanded a new kind of literary medium, one which went beyond the old method of anecdotal reminiscence.

• Amos considered himself different from the old prophetic ways. Amos 7:14 suggests that he had never belonged to any prophetic guild and that he felt there was a divine immediacy to his words which was not true of more commonplace "professional" prophets.

Amos' message/theology:

• Yahweh, Israel's God, is sovereign over the world (4:13; 5:8; 9:2,5).

• Yahweh has a special relationship with Israel.

• Because Israel has broken this relationship, God will destroy her.

Amos reminds his hearers that God will not tolerate an empty shell of religious faith.

A key text: Amos 5:21-24. Scholars argue that this text is one of the most important things Amos had to say.

Hosea: the prophet of Divine Compassion

We know almost nothing about Hosea or about the personal circumstances under which he received and carried out God's call to be a prophet. The brief introduction to the Book (1:1) tells us that he was the son of an otherwise unknown Beeri. It seems that he was born and raised and preached in the

Northern Kingdom (Hosea's favorite word for his nation is Ephraim). The most intriguing and baffling aspect of Hosea's personal life is his relationship with the woman Gomer.

Date of Hosea's Work: c.745-722 B.C.E.

Location: The Northern Kingdom.

Central Theological Concepts: Israel has broken the Covenant which God established with the nation by responding to the faithful love of God with faithlessness. Therefore, God will destroy the nation.

Hosea's message/theology:

• Israel is the people of Yahweh.
• Israel has rejected Yahweh's love and has broken the Covenant by:
>   -disregarding the Laws of the Covenant
>   -compromising God's authority and asking for a king
>   -false worship, mostly the Canaanite fertility deity Baal
• Yahweh is calling Israel to come back. The grounds for the restoration of the Covenant are similar to those expressed by Amos:
>   -steadfast love, kindness
>   -justice
>   -knowledge of God
>   -faithfulness
>   -mercy
• Israel will be punished.
• In Yahweh's love, Israel will someday be restored.

Key texts: (4:1-3) Hosea uses the language of the Law and the courtroom to demand that Israel live up to its legal duty in the Covenant. (6:4) Yet God does not forget Israel nor lose the hope of recovering its love again! (11:8-9: Beautiful soliloquy!)

Such deep feeling for God's love of Israel lends the prophet to picture Yahweh watching over the people like a father over his young in chapter 11, and like a husband in love with an unfaithful wife in chapters 1-3. The source of salvation that clearly comes across here is the divine nature of God, not the political ties with foreign nations.

Isaiah

The material in the book of Isaiah is more than the product of a single individual and includes the work of a "living prophetic tradition," which continued long after the prophet's death and which, to a greater or lesser extent was carried on in his name. In the case of the Isaiah tradition, modern scholarship has been able to identify two additional prophetic personalities beyond that of *Isaiah of Jerusalem*. Because we do not know their names, they are referred to simply as *Second Isaiah* (who lived in Babylon near the end of the Exile) and the *Third Isaiah* (who was active shortly after the restoration of Jerusalem).

Isaiah of Jerusalem   Chapters 1-39

Second Isaiah   Chapters 40-55

Third Isaiah   Chapters 56-66

Isaiah of Jerusalem

Date of Isaiah's Work: c.742-701 B.C.E.

Location: Jerusalem

Central Theological Concepts: A just and holy God demands righteousness and trust from the people. Although the people will be judged, a remnant will be preserved. Furthermore, God will raise up a *universal king from the line of David.*

The Theology of Isaiah 1-39:

- Yahweh is a holy God who demands justice and righteousness from the people
- Sin is rebellion against Yahweh
- Because of love for them, Yahweh calls his people to repent
- The consequence of sin and rebellion against Yahweh is judgment
- Beyond judgment a remnant will be saved (8:18; 10:20-23; 11:11-16)
- A Messiah of the line of David will be raised up

Isaiah, dissatisfied over the performances of the Davidic kings who were his contemporaries, looked to God's raising up a member of the house of David who would surpass such kings as Ahaz and Hezekiah in both faith and power.

The three passages, 7:14-17, 9:1-7, and 11:1-9, have played a central role in shaping the messianic faith of the Christian church.

Ezekiel

Ezekiel was a younger contemporary of Jeremiah. Very little direct information is given about the individual Ezekiel in the book. Ezekiel was a priest, the son of a certain Buzi (1:3). Young Ezekiel probably grew up in Jerusalem and was trained for the priesthood in a school attached to the Temple. The first 13 years of his life coincided with the religious and patriotic enthusiasm which characterized the life of the Temple community, and it was perhaps during those early years that his love for the true and distinctive worship of Yahweh would have been nurtured. As we know from the preaching of Jeremiah (Jer 7:1-20; 26:1-6), this was a period in which the forms of worship were maintained, but were deprived of much of their deeper spiritual and moral content. Ezekiel is probably to be identified with a minority in the priestly community, who, like Jeremiah, saw the disastrous consequences of this hollow religion.

Ezekiel was among the group of Jews who were forced to make the long trek from Jerusalem to Babylon after the first fall of the city. Together with other persons of wealth and rank, he was a part of this first deportation and compelled to begin a new life far from the homeland. Ezekiel lived in the Jewish settlement of Tel-Aviv (3:15). In 592, he experienced a vision of God which gave to his life a new direction.

Date of Ezekiel's Work: From 592 to approximately 571 B.C.E.

Location: Either Jerusalem or Babylon, probably the latter.

Central Theological Concepts: God has not forgotten the Jews exiled to Babylon, but will judge those Jews still living in Judah and will ultimately restore the people.

Ezekiel's theology:

• Yahweh stands in judgment over human sin
• Beyond judgment, Yahweh is with the people, wherever they may be, bringing them life
• Individuals, as well as the nation, have an obligation to respond to the presence of Yahweh, a response which centers upon the commitment of the heart (36:26-27)
• Yahweh's rule over the people will be embodied in a king of the line of David.

Striking features: the language is highly symbolic, the visions are bizarre and so is the behavior. But beyond the unusual symbolism, another element stands out:

> Ezekiel's realization that Yahweh, the God of Israel, is not confined to the land of Judah nor is the worship of Yahweh confined to the Jerusalem Temple. The presence of Yahweh was in Babylon, with the people. Whereas his early ministry pointed to Yahweh's judgment upon Jerusalem, his late ministry emphasizes Yahweh's intention to save and restore this people (37:1-14).

(Notes based on *The Hebrew Prophets* by James D. Newsome, Jr. Atlanta: John Knox Press, 1984)

• The Wisdom Writings

(Notes based on Lawrence Boadt's *Reading the Old Testament*, and *The Catholic Bible (NAB)*, Personal Study Edition)

The wisdom writings of the Old Testament are often over-looked by modern readers which is unfortunate because they reflect Israel's ancient respect for wisdom. The books differ among themselves in both style and subject matter, but they all have in common certain qualities which set them apart from other biblical texts:

1. Not much interest in the great acts of divine salvation proclaimed by the Torah and the prophets
2. Little interest in Israel as a nation or in its history
3. A questioning attitude about the problems of life: why there is suffering, inequality and death, and why the wicked prosper
4. A search for how to master life and understand how humans should behave before God
5. A great interest in the universal human experiences that affect *all* people and not just believers in Yahweh
6. A joy in the contemplation of Creation and God as Creator

These books are:

- Proverbs: an anthology of mostly short sayings in poetical form whose purpose is to teach wisdom for successful living.

- Job: a dramatic poem that treats the problems of suffering of the innocent, and of retribution.

- Ecclesiastes (in Hebrew, *Qoheleth*): a treatise on the vanity, or emptiness, of all things. The book is concerned with the purpose and value of human life.

- Psalms: a collection of 150 prayers in song form.

- Song of Songs (Canticle of Canticles): a collection of love poems full of sensuous imagery. It could be seen as a portrayal of ideal human love.

The following were written in Greek and appear only in the Catholic Bible:

- **Ecclesiasticus** (in Hebrew, *Sirach*): a collection of proverbs dealing with moral instruction, written to show that real wisdom was to be found in the traditions of Israel and not in the godless philosophy of the day.

- **Wisdom of Solomon:** Oratory from the Jewish community of Alexandria about 100 B.C.E.. The author explains traditions and themes familiar to Judaism but reinterprets them from the experience of living in a Hellenistic culture.

VI. "AND THE WORD BECAME FLESH..." *Jn 1*

What is the New Testament?
Who put it together?

• Divisions of the New Testament

The N.T. is divided into four parts and together they include a wide variety of types of literature. In the order in which the books appear in the NT. the four parts are:

1.   **GOSPELS:** Books that tell the story of the life of Jesus. "Gospel" comes from the Anglo-Saxon "god-spell" which means "good tidings." The Greek word, *euangelion* means "good news" (of Jesus Christ).

            Mark (c.70 C.E.)
            Matthew (c.80-85 C.E.)
            Luke (c.80-85 C.E.)   John (c.90-100 C.E.)

2.   **ACTS OF THE APOSTLES**: It is the continuation of Luke's Gospel and it tells the story of the origins of Christianity after the death and resurrection of Jesus through the time of Paul's preaching in Rome --- the period covering approximately 35-64 C.E. It is usually dated after the destruction of Jerusalem in 70 C.E.

3.   **LETTERS:** (21 addressed to a variety of Christian communities and individuals)

A. Seven are **Pauline**, that is, written by Paul around 50-60 C.E.:
> 1 Thessalonians
> 1 & 2 Corinthians
> Philippians
> Philemon
> Galatians
> Romans

B. Three are called Deutero-Pauline. Probably not written by Paul, but by a disciple of Paul (Date uncertain):
> Ephesians
> Colossians
> 2 Thessalonians

C. Three are known as the Pastoral Letters, because they are addressed to pastors of churches. Although they bear Paul's Name, they appear to be later compositions, written after his death (c.110 C.E.):
> 1 & 2 Timothy
> Titus

D. The letter to Hebrews has no named author (c.90 C.E.)

E. Seven other letters are called Apostolic, because they are attributed to Jesus' Apostles (c.60-110 C.E.):
> James
> 1 & 2 Peter
> 1, 2 & 3 John
> Jude

4.   **REVELATION:** (c.90 C.E.): The apocalyptic account of the revelation to a Christian named John.

THE FORMATION OF THE NEW TESTAMENT

1-30 C.E. (First third of the century) JESUS' ERA	30-70 (Second third of the century)	70 - 100 (Last third of the century)	AFTER 100
	THE APOSTOLIC ERA (The great apostles Peter, Paul and James died about the year 60 C.E.)	THE SUB-APOSTOLIC ERA (Second and third generation Christians)	

THE WRITINGS INCORPORATED THE CHRISTIANS' REFLECTIONS ABOUT CHURCH PROBLEMS

30-50	50's	60's	70	70's-80's	90's	
	I-II Thess I-II Cor Galatians Romans	Colossians Ephesians		Acts Hebrews	I-II-III John Revelation	II Peter *Letters of St. Ignatius of Antioch*
					I Clement	
Philippians Philemon?						
		I-II Timothy...............				
		Titus				
		I Peter...............			*Didache*	
		James				
		Jude				

PUBLIC MINISTRY
28 - 30

WRITINGS PROCLAIMING THE WORDS AND DEEDS OF JESUS (GOSPELS)

	Mark	Matthew Luke	John	*Apocryphal gospels*
The preaching continues and the first pre-gospels, now lost, are written				

The Bible is difficult to understand.
How can I read it without getting all confused?

• <u>Tips to remember before reading the New Testament</u>

1. The Bible contains the Word of God, but it is not God!

2. Ask the Holy Spirit to guide you in discovering the message that God intends for you. Do not get lost in "trivia pursuit."

3. The Bible is a book written by believers for believers. It is not a book to study science or the history of the universe. It is the Sacred Book of Christians and it reveals not only God, but the way God was understood throughout the ages.

4. There are diverse literary styles in the books of the New Testament. Do not read them in the same way. Think about a newspaper: comics, headlines and editorials are not the same!

5. Do not get discouraged. The problem of the interpretation of the Bible is not new. The Bible itself bears witness that its interpretation can be a difficult matter. *(See Acts 8:30-35; 2 Peter 1:20, 3:16)*

6. Leave room for Mystery. God is beyond anything that we can read in the pages of the Bible. Learn to be comfortable with the paradoxes of Christianity.

7. For Catholics, the Word of God is Jesus, and is alive. Do not place your trust on "printed" words, but in the living Word of God. Do not allow the "letter" to kill the "spirit."

8.   Studying the Bible is more than memorizing passages. It includes "swallowing" the message and making it our own. *(See Ezekiel 3:1-11)*

Were the New Testament events being recorded as they took place?

• Oral Tradition

The early Christian church originated and existed in an oral culture, thus it employed patterns or forms for remembering and passing on stories about Jesus. We have access to those traditions only through the Gospels. These written documents included and sometimes adapted stories about Jesus from the oral tradition to fit their purposes. Moreover:

- Stories were first told by the Jewish Christians who belonged to the church in Palestine. They told the stories in Aramaic.
- Christianity began to grow mainly in a Greek-speaking Gentile oriented church.

    Therefore:

- Stories were not only translated from Aramaic to Greek, but also were translated from a Semitic to a Hellenistic cultural context.
- Much had already taken place in early Christianity before the Gospels were written.

• The Emergence of Christian Writings

- Christianity began in an oral culture. Hand-written books on hand-made paper were expensive to produce.

- Paul's Letters were meant to be "read" as he gave advice for problems in the early communities.

- In the early years most Christians were convinced that Jesus was going to return from heaven very soon. The end was at hand and preaching the word was more important than writing books that soon no one would need.

- The need of something written to be used in worship or teaching prompted the composition of brief collections of the stories of Jesus.

- As far as it is known, no one before Mark tried to compose a continuous account of the entire life of Jesus.

- The group of Apostles and eyewitnesses who had accompanied Jesus during his ministry was diminishing.

- As time passed and Jesus did not return (*Parousia*), the Christian communities became more interested in preserving the Jesus traditions.

- The expansion and growth of Christianity produced different versions of Christian belief and behavior. Christians felt the need for some standard, other than Apostolic teachings in Jerusalem, to determine the acceptable faith and practice.

- As persecutions increased, some stories of Jesus proved very supportive to sustain those who were suffering.

- As the church became distinct from Judaism, written collections of relevant stories of Jesus were needed.

- There were gaps in the life of Jesus that the early stories did not cover. The imagination of popular Christian piety expanded brief accounts and added fictional fabrications to fill these gaps (e.g., the Gospel of Peter, the Infancy Gospel of Thomas).

- By writing the stories the early church was able to protect them from distortion and addition.

• The Gospel "Genre"

The term "genre" is used to describe a type of literature (e.g., history, short story, poetry, fairy tales, comic books). Knowing the genre of a work helps us to know how to interpret it. The problem with the Gospels is that there was no such genre before these first were written. They are unique among the religious literature of their time. Other ancient genres with which the gospels can be compared are: ancient histories, biographies, and tragic dramas.

Are all Gospels alike?

• The Synoptic Gospels

The first three Gospels in the canon, Matthew, Mark and Luke are called *Synoptic Gospels,* that is, they can be viewed together with *one (syn) look (optic).* Most scholars believe that both Matthew and Luke followed the general outline of Mark's Gospel. The priority of Mark was first suggested at the end of the 18th Century and it is the predominant scholarly hypothesis today.

Scholars also believe that both Matthew and Luke incorporated material from other sources. A *major source used by Luke and Matthew is called "Q," from quelle, the German word for source.* The "Q" source theory was presented by a German scholar in 1838.

- The Two-source Theory

The "Two-Source Theory" of the Synoptic Gospels believes that both Matthew and Luke possessed, while writing their gospels, two main sources:

1. The Gospel of Mark, either in the precise form in which it has come down to us or in a form very similar to our own.

2. A collection of Jesus' sayings, commonly called **"Q."** Originally composed in Aramaic, Q was quickly translated into Greek. Both Matthew and Luke had individual copies of Greek translations.

This basic two-source theory easily breaks down into an uncomplicated four-source proposal since it becomes evident to any Gospel reader that Mt has material peculiar to himself, which derives from neither Mk, Q, nor Lk, and that Lk also has special material not found in the other sources. If we designate Mt's special material as " M" and Lk's as " L" we get the following illustration:

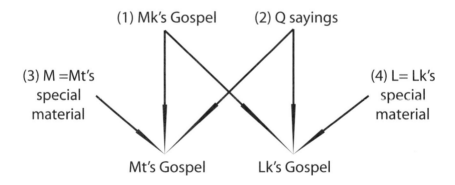

Scholars allude to "the Synoptic Problem," referring to the difficulty in explaining the similarities and differences in these three Gospels as it concerns order and content.

(Adapted from *Mark, Matthew, Luke: a Guide to the Gospel Parallels* by Neal M. Flanagan, OSM, The Liturgical Press, Collegeville, MN, 1978)

- The Three Levels of the Gospels

III. "SACRED AUTHORS"

THIRD LEVEL *(Sitz im Euangelium):* Describes the Gospel material in its ultimate stage, as **it exists now in the four Gospels**. In this stage, the words of Christ, which were originally preached by him to a limited Jewish audience and were later preached by the Apostles to a wider but still limited audience throughout the Roman Empire, are now synthesized and organized into written documents which bear the personal impress of their authors, the four inspired evangelists.

II. "THE APOSTLES"

SECOND LEVEL *(Sitz im Leben Kirche):* Describes these same events and sayings of Christ's life as they came to be preached by the Apostles and others and adapted to the moral, dogmatic, and catechetical needs of the early Apostolic Church. In this stage the sayings of Jesus and the events of his life are not distorted nor destroyed, but they **are adapted** to the needs of new audiences who have never seen or heard him. They are adapted also to new situations and new problems which did not exist during the ministry of Christ.

I. "CHRIST OUR LORD"

FIRST LEVEL *(Sitz im Leben Christ):* Describes the Gospel material in its most primitive form; namely, **the actual events of Jesus' life and the words preached by him during his ministry in Palestine.** Original sayings and actual events, this level provides the historical and theological bedrock of the Gospel materials.

A simple reporting of things to be remembered would require that chronological order be followed and that words be quoted literally. A preached version of the same would allow the author the liberty of sometimes changing the chronological order and quoting freely as long as he preserved the sense of the words or the content of the doctrine. Such liberties, which certainly were taken by the evangelists, do not destroy the fundamental historicity of the Gospels.

(Notes from "The Historicity of the Gospels," in *Matthew: his mind and his message*, by Peter Ellis. The Liturgical Press, Collegeville, MN, 1974)

Are all the stories in the gospels the same?
Are they all parables?

• <u>Some types of stories</u>

1. The Pronouncement Story - **Mk 2:15-17**
   15: Setting   16: action   17: Significant saying

2. The Miracle Story - **Mk 1:29-31**
      29: Description of need   31a: Miraculous act
      31b: Results

3. Stories about Christ (legends, myths)

   <u>Legend</u>: Refers to stories about holy people and religious heroes. They are meant to be read for inspiration, instruction, and spiritual edification.
   <u>Myth:</u> The technical meaning is a narrative expression of an idea foundational to human existence which can be known, experienced, and appropriated repeatedly by way of recitation and ritual. Scholars include in this category those stories which emphasize the identity of Jesus as the Christ of God.

Examples: Infancy narratives, the story of the twelve-year-old Jesus in the Temple, his baptism by John the Baptist, the temptation, the transfiguration, the triumphal entry into Jerusalem, and so on.

4. Sayings of the Lord (some examples)

Independent sayings of Jesus which have no narrative setting or framework: *Mk 4:21-25*

- *"Logia"* or *wisdom* sayings: Mk 3:24-25; 7:15; 9:50; 11:24-25; Mt 6:23; Lk 6:27-31
- *Prophetic and Apocalyptic* sayings: Lk 6:24-25; 12:35-58; 21:34-36; Mk 13:12-13; 13:1-2, 5-37; Mt 23:13-39; 25:1-13
- *Legal* sayings and *community rules:* Mk 11:25; 3:28-29; 10:11-12; Mt 18:15-17; 5:17-48; 18:19-20; Lk 10:2-16
- *The "I"* sayings of Jesus or *Christological* sayings: Lk 12:49-51; 9:23; 19:10; Mt 5:17; 12:40; Mk 8:38; 9:41
- The *Parable*: A brief story which dramatizes a common human experience from which it draws its comparison or analogy. The entire story is directed to a single, central point. When the point is grasped the parable has accomplished its didactic purpose. The rest of the detail is secondary in importance.

- <u>Small Group Work</u>

Read Lk 15:3-10

What is the common human experience?

What is the central point?

When we divert attention from the central point by focusing too much attention on secondary details, we convert the parable into an allegory. Allegory is not analogical but rather finds hidden, special meaning in all details. Mk 4:13-20 gives an allegorical interpretation of the parable of the seed and the soils.

<u>Note</u>: The conviction of the first Christians that Jesus was the Messiah sent by God colored the stories about Jesus which they told. At any given moment in early Christianity it was the condition of the contemporary Christian community and the challenges it was facing at that time which determined the context from which Jesus was viewed and to which the Jesus tradition was adapted.

(Notes adapted from Keith F. Nickle's *The Synoptic Gospels*, Atlanta: SCM Press Ltd., 1981, and *The Interpretation of the Bible in the Church*, Pontifical Biblical Commission, 1993)

• The Gospel according to Mark

Author. The first and shortest Gospel does not tell us about the author. Church tradition as far back as early in the 2nd Century, has attributed it to Mark. Around 130 C.E, a Christian named Papias stated that Mark was an associate and interpreter of Peter (See Acts 12:112; 1 Pet 5:13) who wrote down what he remembered of the Lord's words and deeds. *(In Acts 10:36-43, Peter's words to Cornelius are Mark's Gospel in miniature).* Mark wrote in a simple, popular style. He is a great storyteller and does not include long speeches.

Place and time of composition. Accepted by the majority of scholars as the first to be written, most likely in Rome. The "martyr" spirit of the Christians in Mark fits Rome in the 60's, time of Nero's persecutions, just before the destruction of Jerusalem by the Roman legions around 70 C.E. Therefore, the Gospel is placed in the late 60's. A Roman origin would explain the rapid circulation of the Gospel, which put copies of it in the hands of both Matthew and Luke within one-two decades.

Purpose. Mark wrote to be of service to his own community which would have been subject to both Jewish and Gentile influences. His primary purpose was to strengthen his community's faith in Jesus as the Christ, the resurrected Son of God.

Mark's Jesus. A man in a hurry. No stories of his birth or childhood or young adulthood. Before the first chapter ends, Jesus has called the first disciples, performed his first cure and set off for Capernaum. He is earthy, easy to relate to, and approachable. He shows a wide range of emotions which make him the most human Jesus of the four Gospels.

Mark reflected his understanding of who Jesus was in the titles which he used to refer to him in his Gospel:

Rabbi = Teacher

Christ = Greek translation of the Hebrew "Messiah"

Son of Man = Rooted in Jewish religious traditions. Its Jewish heritage made it expressive of a more than human figure who will come in power and glory at the end of the world (Mk 8:38; 13:26; 14:62). Mark was concerned with the identity of Jesus and he used this title to convey not only Jesus' glory and authority, but his rejection, suffering, death and resurrection. (See Mk 8:31; 9:31; 10:33-34)

Son of God = Used at the beginning (1:1) and at the end (15:39). For Mark this title expressed Jesus' unique relationship to God. The identity of Jesus as Son of God was incontestable. (See 3:11; 1:11; 9:7; 15:39)

Key elements in the Gospel.

1. Repeated use of the word *immediately* creates a sense of urgency.
2. When Jesus performs a miracle, he instructs the person **not to say anything**. This is known as the *Messianic Secret.*
3. The disciples, especially Peter, do not understand Jesus' words and actions.
4. Peter (at Caesarea Philippi) and the Centurion (at the foot of the cross) recognize Jesus as the anointed One (Messiah), and Son of God.
5. Jesus is very human, filled with human emotions, and always in a hurry.

The Gospel develops in three stages:

- Chapters 1-8: Readers are drawn into a relationship with a powerful healer and preacher. No one seems to understand!
- Chapters 9-15: Reveal to the readers the meaning of true Christian discipleship (Summed up in 10:45).
- Chapters 16:6ff. The Gospel continues in the life of the Church, until the risen Lord comes again.

- The Gospel according to Matthew

Author. The Gospel itself does not identify its author. Its attribution to Matthew is a second-century tradition that says that Matthew, the tax-collector, wrote down the words of Jesus in Aramaic. The present author was perhaps inspired by him. Modern scholars agree that he was a Jewish Christian, strongly in favor of the mission to the Gentiles with which the book both begins (Magi of chap.2), and ends (Great Commission of 28:18-20).

Place and time of composition. Matthew wrote in Greek, about 85 C.E., in the communities of Syria and Palestine, perhaps at Antioch.

Purpose. Matthew's communities seem to have been composed above all of Jewish Christians, but also open to Gentiles. He wrote at a time when the relationships between Jews and Christians had changed dramatically. For Matthew's community, this is a time of great confusion and pain as they experienced a breakdown in their relationship with their past and a need to launch a new understanding of themselves as people of God and followers of the Messiah.

While Jesus himself did not seek to establish a Christian church separate from Judaism, Mt 13:54 - 19:1 describes what the life of the community of believers (*ecclesia*) will be like in anticipation of the coming of the Reign of God.

Matthew's Jesus. Unlike Mark, Matthew is very interested in Jesus' origins. His genealogy covers Joseph's lineage which is in keeping with his tendency to make Joseph the central figure of the infancy narrative. Matthew presents Jesus as the new Moses, the Teacher. He is the fulfillment of Old Testament Law and the authority and teaching of God are found in Jesus, the Christ. While Mark's Jesus has much to SHOW us, Matthew's Jesus has much to TELL us.

Key elements in the Gospel

1. Matthew is a teacher. He rearranges the words of Jesus into five great speeches, doubtless in order to present him as the new Moses. He abbreviates the miracle stories, often keeping two figures, Jesus and the person concerned; the stories lose their vividness but make a greater impact as teaching.

2. Matthew is the only Gospel to use the word church, not buildings or institutions, but the Greek word *ecclesia*, meaning "assembly."

3. Matthew portrays the disciples in a more favorable light than Mark. They are no longer the ignorant, dense people. He presents Peter as a model disciple and considers it "OK" to be a fallible disciple.

4. Matthew refers to the Jewish Scriptures more than 130 times. It is the Gospel which has the strongest Jewish flavor.

5. A distinctive feature of this Gospel is the use of "promise and fulfillment" formulae to introduce quotations from the Hebrew Scriptures. The formula reads like: *"such and such an event in the life of Jesus took place in order to fulfill what the prophet had said."*

There are twelve of these quotations:

Mt 1:22-23; 2:5-6, 15, 17-18, 23; 4:14-16; 8:17; 12:17-21; 3:14-15, 35; 21:4-5; 27:9-10

(See also 3:3-4; 11:10; 15:7-9; 26:56)

The five great speeches or discourses in Matthew

Book 1. The Proclamation of the Reign (3:1-7:29)
   A. Narrative Section: The Beginning of the Ministry (3:1-4:25)
   B. Discourse: The Sermon on the Mount (5:1-7:29)

Book 2. Ministry in Galilee (8:1-11:1)
   A. Narrative Section: Cycle of Ten Miracles (8:1-9:34)
   B. Discourse: The Missionary Sermon (9:35-11:1)

Book 3. Controversy and Parables (11:2-13:52)
   A. Narrative Section: incredulity and hostility of the Jews (11:2-12:50)
   B. Discourse: The Parables of the Reign (13-1-52)

Book 4. The Formation of the Disciples (13:53-18:35)
   A. Narrative Section: various episodes preceding the journey to Jerusalem (13:53-17:27)
   B. Discourse: The Sermon on Christian community living (the church). (18:1-35)

Book 5. Judea and Jerusalem (19:1-25:46)
   A. Narrative Section: Journey to Jerusalem and events there (19:1-23:39)
   B. Discourse: The Eschatological (end time) Sermon (24:1-25:46)

- ### The Infancy Narratives according to Matthew

- ▪ Joseph is the main character in the Infancy Narrative (1:1-2:23)

- ○ The Messianic genealogy comes through Joseph (1:1-16)
- ○ A messenger of God appears to Joseph in a dream (1:19-23)
- ○ As the legal son of Joseph, Jesus will be called the "son of David" (1:24-25)
- ○ Wise men from the East who possess astronomical and astrological knowledge worship Jesus at Bethlehem. The faith of the Gentile wise men stands in contrast to the cynical cunning of Herod (2:1-12)
- ○ The flight into Egypt occurs because an angel of the Lord appears to Joseph in a dream (2:13-18)
- ○ The family returns to Nazareth because the angel appears again to Joseph in a dream (2:19-23)

- ### The Gospel according to Luke

(Notes taken from *The New Jerome Bible Handbook*. Collegeville, MN: The Liturgical Press, 1993)

Author. Since the second century Luke has been seen as the "beloved physician" (Col 4:14) who accompanied Paul from Troas to Philippi. From his introduction to the Gospel, we know that he was not an eye-witness to Jesus' life, nor one of the Apostles.

Place and time of composition. Luke 21:5-38 presupposes that Jerusalem has been destroyed; thus he wrote after 70 C.E. Luke, who also wrote the Acts of the Apostles, does not reflect knowledge of the bitter persecution of Christians around 90 C.E. Thus, one arrives at a Date of 80-85 for the composition of Luke-Acts, a two-volume work. Some scholars have suggested Rome as the place of composition, others Antioch. All we know for sure is that he wrote for a Greek speaking, Gentile Christian community with well-to-do members who were rethinking their mission in a hostile environment.

Purpose. "The key question of Luke's communities is this: if God has not been faithful to the promises made to God's chosen people and has allowed their Holy City and Temple to be destroyed, what reason do Gentile Christians have to think that God will be faithful to promises made to them?" Through the two books Luke-Acts, the author demonstrates that God is faithful in unexpected ways, now to include Gentiles, the poor, the outcasts, women, tax collectors, as well as the Jews who have accepted Jesus as the Chosen One.

Luke's Jesus. Luke presents a compassionate, forgiving, gentle Jesus. He is constantly praying, especially before an important event: his baptism, the selection of the Twelve Apostles, Peter's confession, the Transfiguration, the teaching of the Lord's Prayer, the Garden scene. Luke is repelled by violence, strong language, and raw emotion, thus he often softens these when he uses Mark as source material. Luke's Jesus is surrounded by an aura of kindness and peace even amid painful events, such as the crucifixion and death.

There is a final quality in Luke's Jesus, and this is the faithfulness of Jesus' God. Luke begins the Gospel telling how promises have been fulfilled in the birth of Jesus, and he ends telling how God has fulfilled promises in rising Jesus from the dead.

Key elements in the Gospel.

1.   Luke's Gospel is universal. His genealogy of Jesus extends back to Adam (3:23-38).

2.   His understanding of God's plan of salvation includes

all: Jews and Gentiles, rich and poor, men and women. Women play a prominent role in Luke's Gospel. He also shows a special concern for sinners.

3. The Gospel gives great importance to the role of the Holy Spirit and to prayer. Luke describes all important actions, including Jesus' actions, as prompted by the Spirit. It has been called by some the *Gospel of the Holy Spirit*.

4. Luke understood his work to be an organized history as his own introduction testifies. The Gospel is organized in such a way that everything points toward Jerusalem and the events that will happen there (also called the "travel narrative," 9:51-19:27).

• <u>The Infancy Narratives according to Luke</u>

▪ Mary is the main character in the Infancy Narrative

◦ The story of the birth of Jesus is very different from Matthew's. The emphasis is on Mary, Elizabeth and Zechariah, not on Joseph. The story does not mention the Magi. Instead, he includes the shepherds from the nearby fields, consistent with his interest in the poor and the marginalized from society.
◦ The angel announces the birth of John the Baptist: 1:5-25
◦ Gabriel's annunciation to Mary: 1:26-38
◦ Mary visits Elizabeth and Elizabeth is filled with the Holy Spirit: 1:39-45
◦ The *Magnificat* (Mary's Song): 1:46-55
◦ John the Baptist: 1:57-80
◦ The birth of Jesus (journey to Bethlehem, shepherds and angels): 2:1-21
◦ The presentation of Jesus and the purification of Mary in the Temple: 2:21-36
◦ Jesus lost in the Temple: 2:41-52

Other highlights of the Gospel:

- God's promises fulfilled in Jesus: 4:16-30
- Jesus' mission is for sinners: 5:27-32
- The Sabbath is subordinate to Jesus and his compassion: 6:1-11
- The Parables of Mercy: 15:1-32
- Women as evangelists: 23:56b-24:12
- Emmaus: 24:13-35

- <u>Small Group Work</u>

1. Read Mark 10:35-45. What are James and John asking of Jesus? What does Jesus promise them? What can we learn today from this story?

2. Make a list of the titles given to Jesus in the first two chapters of the Gospel of Mark and the context in which the title is given. In your opinion,

   a) Who did people think Jesus was?

   b) Who did Mark think Jesus was?

3.   Read Matthew 13:3b-23. What is the message/point of this parable?

4.   Identify and explain the different beginnings of the three synoptic gospels. What can we learn from this study?

5.   Read Luke 8:1-3. What do you learn about discipleship from this account?

6.   Read Luke 10:1-17. What are the characteristics of disciples and their mission?

THE FOUR FACES OF JESUS

*Mark's
harried, hurried,
human Jesus*

*Matthew's
new Moses:
Jesus the Teacher*

*Luke's
compassionate,
forgiving Jesus*

*John's noble,
majestic,
divine Jesus*

Who is Jesus for you?

- <u>Small Group Work</u>

The Gospel for our times

Jesus taught primarily using parables. Side by side with his teaching, Jesus' miracles gave expression to the manifestation of the Reign of God in time.

Imagine that you have been given the task of writing the Christian message in an abbreviated form. You have to be brief and clear in your presentation of the Good News of Jesus Christ to your particular community. What passage from the Gospels would you select and why? Would you use parables, miracles stories, other stories?

Passage

Reason

What were the first communities like?
Was there any conflict among members?

- ## The Acts of the Apostles

The Acts of the Apostles is the second of two volumes attributed to Luke—perhaps Luke, the physician and companion
of Paul, who is mentioned in Colossians 4:14, Philemon 24,
and 2 Timothy 4:11.

This second volume is a "history" of the development of the
Christian church from the resurrection of Jesus in Jerusalem
to Paul's arrival in Rome.

Acts does not give us an accurate history of the life and deeds
of Paul, but the author's interpretation of the significance of
Paul's life and deeds. It attempts to explain the spread of
Christianity beyond the bounds of Judaism.

Luke does not seem to know Hebrew. He used the Greek
translation as he wrote his Gospel and Acts in Greek. His use
of the Greek Bible was important:

- Jewish rabbis of the first centuries treated their
  Bible as Law
- Luke and other Christians saw it primarily as
  prophecy
- The Law approach looked to the Old Testament
  for guidelines and rules of how to live in the daily
  aspects of one's life
- Christians searched the Jewish Scriptures for
  prophecies of the Messiah and end times of fulfillment

Thus, Luke viewed Moses not as the "Lawgiver" but as the "Prophet."

Speeches make up a large part of Acts. The three most important kinds are:

1. Missionary speeches to convert Jews or Gentiles

2. Defense speeches in the trials of Paul

3. The Farewell speech in Acts 20

• <u>Small Group Work</u>

1.   Read Acts 1 and 2. What happened at Pentecost? How does the speech in Acts 2 explain the Pentecost event?

2.   Read Acts 9:1-30. Explain Paul's conversion.

3.   Read Acts 13. Explain Paul's Gentile missionary work and his understanding of the relationship between Judaism and Christianity.

4.   Read Acts 15. What was the problem that prompted Paul and Barnabas to go to Jerusalem? How was it solved?

5.   Read Acts 26. Explain the importance of Paul's speech.

*How is the Gospel according to John
different from the Synoptics?*

- <u>The Gospel of John</u>

Christ, the divine Word of God (Logos), became human.

The Gospel of John is especially attractive to the thinking person and has been called "the Spiritual Gospel" since the second century. Unlike Matthew, Mark and Luke, which present comprehensive and similar (synoptic) overviews of Jesus' life, John is a highly stylized arrangement of carefully selected events and words, all directed toward one major purpose: *that readers might find life by believing in Jesus as the Christ.*

The evangelist's identity has never been deciphered. Scholars are almost unanimous in holding that the Fourth Evangelist was not John the son of Zebedee. Today, it seems best to accept the Beloved Disciple as anonymous, who was, in all probability, an eyewitness companion of the earthly Jesus but not one of the Twelve. The Gospel is believed to have been written in the 90's.

The Jesus tradition (the gospel) as remembered, interpreted, and transmitted by the Beloved Disciple was authoritative for the Johannine community and the basis of the written Gospel.

• <u>The Prologue (1:1-18)</u> states briefly what the whole of the Gospel will spell out over twenty-one chapters. It has both, structure and content.

A. Structure: Partially determined by the presentation of "Wisdom personified" in the Old Testament books. There, as in *Wisdom 9:9-12 or Proverbs 8:22-36*, Wisdom is first with God, then shares in Creation, will come to earth, and there gift humankind.

B. Content: These eighteen verses speak of God's revelation, of how God has explained himself to us. God through the centuries has self-revealed through Creation (vv.2-5), through the Old Testament word (vv.10-13), that is, through his covenants, the Mosaic writings, the prophets, and the wisdom literature. Those who believed in the ancient revelation became "children of God...begotten...by God" (vv.12-13). According to John, God has finally revealed himself to the utmost through the incarnation of the Word, in whom God's glory and presence stand as a sign of his enduring love (v.14). **The Greek text tells us that the Word "pitched his tent"** among us, a striking reference to God's Old Testament presence in the tent-tabernacle during Moses' wanderings with Israel in the desert.

John is not interested in giving us historical facts about the earthly Jesus, but to help us believe that Jesus is the Messiah, the Son of God, the expected Savior of Israel. This position caused a painful and bitter separation between the Johannine community of the late First Century and the Jewish community from which many members of John's community came, and also situates Jesus as both the product of and the fulfillment of the revelation tradition of ancient Israel.

The Johannine Jesus cannot be understood apart from the Hebrew Scriptures, which for John have become the Old Testament, and the background of a new revelation in Jesus.

By the time the Fourth Gospel was written, around 100 C.E., the Christian church had become a faith community distinct from Judaism and had come to believe that Jesus was truly and fully divine.

The seeds for the Theological development of the doctrine of the Trinity are found in the most explicit form in John's Gospel. Jesus is the personal manifestation of God in this world. In Jesus, the Word of God, holy Sophia or Wisdom in the Old Testament, through whom and in whom God created all things, became incarnate (Jn 1:14).

- Testimonies (1:19-51): a whole list of witnesses to Jesus, who, one by one, identify Jesus for John's readers:

  vv. 19-28, vv.29-34, vv.35-39 ,vv.40-42, vv.43-51

- Cana's miracle (2:1-11): "His disciples believed in him." (2:11)

By the end of chapter 1 the Johannine disciples seem to know everything there is to know about Jesus, even his divinity. This is very different from Mark's gospel, in which the disciples come to their faith-knowledge of Jesus only hesitantly, timidly, and imperfectly-and that over a lengthy period of time.

- Main divisions:

  A. The Prologue (1:1-18)

  B. The Book of Signs (Jn 2:1-12:50)

  Seven Signs: Turns water into wine (2:1-12)
  Heals a nobleman's son (4:46-54)
  Heals a lame man at the pool of Bethesda (5:1-17)
  Feeds 5,000 (6:1-14)

Walks on water, stills a storm (6:15-21)
Heals a man blind from birth (9:1-41)
Raises Lazarus from the dead (11:17-45)

C. The Book of Glory (Jn 13:1-20:31)

A Model of Servant-Leadership: Jesus washes
the disciples' feet (13:1-20)
A new Commandment (13:31-35)
The promise of the Paraclete (14:16-18)
The work of the Spirit (16:1-15)
Prayer for his followers (17:1-25)
The Resurrection: skeptics are welcome
(20:24-29)
The purpose of John's Gospel (20:30-31): "that
you may come to believe"

D. Epilogue (21:1-25): Appearance in Galilee

- Other individuals encounter Christ

Andrew (1:40)
Mary of Bethany (11:1)
Nathaniel (1:46)
Lazarus (11:1-44)
Nicodemus (3:1-21)
A Samaritan woman (4:5-29)
Judas (13:21-30)
The women around Jesus (19:25)

In the Fourth Gospel Jesus is the full revelation of a loving
and compassionate God who invites us to know this truth so
that we can be free (8:31-32).

Read Jn 8:57-58
Ex 3:13-14

Read the **I AM** passages in John's Gospel:

> Jn 6:48 I AM the bread of life
>
> 9:5   I AM the light of the world
>
> 10:7   I AM the sheepgate
>
> 10:11   I AM the good shepherd
>
> 11:25   I AM the resurrection and the life
>
> 13:19   I tell you this now, before it takes place, so that when it takes place you may believe that I AM
>
> 14:6   I AM the way, and the truth, and the life
>
> 15:1   I AM the true vine
>
> 15:5   I AM the vine, you are the branches
>
> 18:4-5 Jesus the Nazorean..... I AM

(Some notes taken from Sandra M Schneiders, *Written That You May Believe*. New York: The Crossroad Publishing Co., 1999)

- <u>Small Group Work</u>

1. Peter:

Jesus commissions Peter (21:15-23) "Forgiveness abounds"

Review Mt 16:19 "the keys of the kingdom..."
Jn 18:10   "the defender of Christ..."
Jn 18:15-18, 25-27 "the denial..."
Jn 13:31-38   "What Jesus had predicted about Peter came true..."

How do you think Peter felt after his denial? Maybe disqualified from further service for the Lord?

How do you think he felt when Jesus reconnected with him and called him to authentic love?

2. Read Jn 21:24-25. "there are also many other things that Jesus did...." What does this ending tell you?

What was the purpose of the letters in the New Testament? Did Paul write them all?

• <u>New Testament Letters</u>

There are 21 letters addressed to a variety of Christian communities and individuals:

A. **Seven are Pauline**, that is, written by Paul around 50-60 C.E.
       1 Thessalonians
       1 & 2 Corinthians
       Philippians
       Philemon
       Galatians
       Romans

B. **Three are called Deutero-Pauline**. Probably not written by Paul, but by a disciple of Paul (Date uncertain):
       Ephesians
       Colossians
       2 Thessalonians

C. **Three are known as the Pastoral Letters**, because they are addressed to pastors of churches. Although they bear Paul's name, they appear to be later compositions, written after his death (c.110 C.E.):
       1 & 2 Timothy
       Titus

D. **The letter to Hebrews** has no named author (c.90 C.E.)

E.   **Seven other letters are called Apostolic**, because they are attributed to Jesus' Apostles
(c.60-110 C.E.):

James
1 & 2 Peter
1, 2 & 3 John
Jude

Is it true that the Letter to the Romans
speaks of salvation by faith alone?

• The Letter to the Romans

The data in Romans 15 indicates that Paul wrote it toward the
end of his 3rd mission, shortly before he returned to Jerusalem
in the Spring of 58 C.E. He probably wrote it in Corinth. The
Pauline authorship of Romans is almost universally admit-
ted today, just as it was in antiquity. Paul did not found the

Roman church. It seems that it was established by members of the Jewish-Christian community in Jerusalem who had traveled to Rome. Converts multiplied, and the church to whom Paul sent this letter was predominantly Gentile-Christian.

After years of preaching the Gospel in the eastern Mediterranean area (Rom 15:19), Paul turned to the west, especially Spain. En route he planned to visit Rome to fulfill the desire of years (Rom 1:13; 15:22, 24). But before heading west, he had to carry personally to Jerusalem the collection taken up in the Gentile churches that he had founded (Rom 15:25; cf. 1 Cor 16:1). For this was to manifest to the Jewish-Christian mother church the solidarity existing between the "poor" of the community and the Gentile Christians of Galatia, Macedonia, and Achaia.

Before he departed from Corinth for Jerusalem, he wrote to the Roman church to announce his impending visit. Writing as "the Apostle of the Gentiles" (11:13), he wanted to introduce himself to a community which for the most part did not know him personally. History records that Paul was arrested in Jerusalem, imprisoned in Caesarea for two years, and finally arrived in Rome around 60-61 C.E., some three or four years after his letter had arrived.

Romans is not a summary of Christian doctrine. Some of Paul's teachings on the Church, the Eucharist, the resurrection of the body, eschatology, etc., are missing from it. Rather, **it is a presentation of his missionary reflections on the historic possibility of salvation now offered to all peoples in the good news of Jesus Christ.**

Romans has affected later Christian theology more than any other NT book. Its influence is seen in other NT writings, sub-apostolic compositions, and it played a central role in the Reformation debates. Rom 3:21-4:25 is one of the foremost readings used in ecumenical circles to understand the concept of "salvation through faith alone." Also, Rom 9-11 stands at the heart of contemporary Jewish-Christian dialogue.

Religious situation: In the light of his eastern apostolate, and especially of the Judaizing crisis, Paul came to realize that *the person's justification and salvation depended not on the "deeds of the Law," but on faith in Christ Jesus. Through faith one shares in the effects of the plan of salvation conceived by the Father and brought to realization in the death and resurrection of Jesus.*

(Notes adapted from, *The Collegeville Bible Commentary*, Collegeville, MN, 1983, and *The Jerome Biblical Commentary*, New Jersey: Prentice-Hall, Inc., 1968)

• The First and Second Letters of Paul to the Corinthians

The letters were written by Paul about 56-58 C.E. At the time, Corinth was probably the leading Greek city, large and wealthy. Because of its location, goods and people from around the world flowed in and out of its ports. It was a center for art, philosophy and religion. It contained a number of pagan temples including large ones to Apollo and Aphrodite. The city had a reputation for vice, immorality and debauchery.

Paul went to Corinth around 50 C.E. during his second missionary journey. He is recorded to have stayed there longer (18 months according to Acts 18:11) than in any other place he evangelized. He was not an itinerant among them, but had shared experiences, intimacies, strains and disappointments with its people.

In Corinth, Paul first tried to evangelize the Jewish population, teaching in the synagogue and enjoying some success (Acts 18:1-4). He lived and worked with Aquila and Priscilla, his Jewish-Christian friends who were part of his missionary team there. After being continually assaulted by the Jews (Acts 18:5-6, 12-17), Paul reviewed his priorities. He stopped concentrating on the Jews and focused on the Gentile mission for which he was affirmed by a vision of the Lord (18:7-10). Paul crossed paths with Apollos, who had been instructed by Aquila and Priscilla. Later Apollos himself preached in Corinth. Apollos' eloquence (Acts 18:24) is contrasted with Paul's fear (1 Cor 2:3). There was a certain amount of competition among the followers of Paul and those of Apollos (cf. 1 Cor 9:1-18; 2 Cor 10:1-13:21).

1 Corinthians: Seduction by the surrounding pagan culture had led the Corinthian church into a variety of problems. Thus, 1 Corinthians is full of information about how a Christian lifestyle differs from that of the culture as a whole.

2 Corinthians: This letter, more than any other, allows us to see inside Paul: his passion for the Gospel, his deep love for his churches, the pain he felt over misunderstanding, rejection and attack, and the extent of his sufferings.

- Small Group Work

1. Read Romans 6:1 - 7:6. What is the meaning of baptism in this passage?

2. Read Romans 3:21-4:25. What is your understanding of "salvation through faith alone"?

3. Compare your experience of the Christian life with Paul's description in Rom 5:1-11. Are they similar? How do they differ?

4. Read Romans 7 & 8.
   a) Can you see yourself in chapter 7?
   b) Is there any hope for us?
   c) What does Rom 8:31-39 say to you?

5. Read 1 Cor 1:1-4:21.
   a) What is the situation in Corinth which Paul addresses in the opening of this letter? Where did he get his information?
   b) According to 2:10, what is the role of the Spirit?

6.   Read 1 Cor 15. How does it help you to understand the doctrine of the Resurrection?

7.   Read 1 Cor 11:17-33.
   a)   What does Paul say about the behavior of those gathered for Eucharist?
   b)   What did he mean by "Body of Christ"?
   c)   What does it say to us today?

8.   Read 1 Cor 12 & 13.
   a) What does Paul say about people who claim to have charismatic gifts such as speaking in tongues?
   b) What is the greatest gift according to Paul?

9.   Read 2 Cor 4:7.
   Do you ever feel like a plain old clay pot? What can this passage say to you?

10.   Look at the following problem of First-Century Christians:
   Divisions over personalities and doctrine (1 Cor 1:10-17). Have you ever experienced anything similar in your community?

(Notes from: *The Word in Life Study Bible, NRSV; Catholic Serendipity Bible, NAB; Collegeville Bible Commentary, #7*).

What do the letters say about Jesus' divinity?

• The Letters to the Philippians, Ephesians, Colossians and Hebrews

We Believe in Jesus the Christ...

Christians believe in a Trinitarian God who has been revealed in Jesus Christ. Christians are the only ones who identify Jesus of Nazareth as God. "True God of true God...one in being with the Father." (Creed) Jesus is a historical figure. Christ is the Christian way of looking at Jesus which we call faith.

In the New Testament most of the texts that speak about Jesus are liturgical texts. In the beginning of the Church, the Church's acknowledgment of Jesus' divinity in prayer and liturgy was more important than the teaching of dogmas. The Christological hymns that appear in the letters of Paul are a good example of these liturgical texts. The Church sang to the Lord before making dogmas explicit.

The Christ-hymn	Philippians 2:6-11
Christ, the head of	
the body, the Church	Colossians 1:15-20
Spiritual blessings in Christ	Ephesians 1:3-14
The priesthood of Christ	Hebrews 1:1-5; 2:1-18; 7:1-28

In the year 110 C.E. a Roman report to the emperor read as follows: "They (Christians) gather on a particular day before sunrise, and sing hymns to Christ as God." (Plinius, #96) **This declaration, Christ as God, summarized their entire creed.**

• The Letter to the Philippians

Philippi was a leading town in the Roman province of Macedonia. In Philippi, Paul began the European phase of his missionary work c.50 C.E. on his second mission journey. It is agreed that Paul wrote this letter himself, c.57-58 C.E. It shows Paul at his pastoral best: he praises the congregation, teaches, encourages, admonishes and warns, but always with a clear love for the members.

Women played a leading role in the community from the start: Lydia (Acts 16:14-15, 40); Euodia and Syntyche (Phil 4:2-3). Personal names appearing in the letter suggest that the community was predominantly Gentile Christian.

• The Letter to the Colossians

In many ways the Letter to the Colossians is a mysterious document. We do not know precisely who the author is, nor do we have a clear picture of the doctrines of the false teachers that the author is arguing against. The language of the Letter contains many words which Paul never used and the style is very different from Paul's. It was probably composed after Paul's lifetime, between 70 and 80 C.E., by someone who knew Paul's teaching.

The purpose of Colossians was to bolster the faith of the community (1:3-14; 2:2-3) and to correct errors reported about the church (2:4, 8, 16, 18-22).

Like the Christ hymn of Phil 2:6-11, Col 1:15-20 is one of the most important Theological statements about the person of Christ in the New Testament. Christ is praised as the icon or image of the invisible God, that is, he manifests God's presence in his person. He is called the first-born of all Creation because everything else was created though his mediation. Therefore, he existed before all Creation.

• <u>The Letter to the Ephesians</u>

Most modern scholars believe that Paul did not write the letter, but that one of his disciples who knew Paul's letters very well expanded it or finished it. He probably belonged to a group of followers of Paul that was committed to his thinking and the traditions that had developed in Pauline mission areas. Ephesians was probably written around 80-100 B.C.

While the Letter to the Ephesians shares an interest with Colossians in the portrayal of the cosmic Christ, Ephesians is unique among N.T. writings for its description of the church as one, holy, Catholic, and Apostolic. It is this teaching on the nature of the church that is the key contribution of Ephesians.

Although Ephesians is like a letter in structure, it is more of a Theological lecture, destined for several churches in the Roman province of Asia. It talks of the exaltation of Christ and the church over all heavenly and earthly powers and the reconciliation of Jews and Gentiles in the church under the headship of Christ. It encourages both groups to celebrate their unity.

• <u>Hebrews</u>

Hebrews is one of the best written works of early Christianity. Modern scholars agree that the work is not a letter, it is not by St. Paul, and it is not addressed to "Hebrews." Hebrews is a written sermon, and it is important as one of the earliest Christian sermons on record.

Many commentators favor a date later than the destruction of the Temple in 70 C.E., usually 80-90 C.E. The author wishes to show that the sacrifice of Jesus has replaced Old Testament sacrificial worship. He was a Greek Christian. Apollos, an associate of Paul (see Acts 18:24-28), has been suggested as a possible author. Pleas not to abandon the Christian faith are important parts of this work: 2:1-3; 3:12; 6:4-6.

Hebrews has some ideas in common with the First Letter of Peter, which purports to come from Rome. Even more significantly, it is closely related to the non-biblical First Letter of Clement, the reputed bishop of Rome near the end of the first century. These contacts suggest that Hebrews shared a kind of Roman theology and was most likely written from Rome.

Major theme: the priesthood of Christ. Hebrews is a self-contained theology of salvation in Christ. It does not lay emphasis on the resurrection or on the Eucharist. Instead, Hebrews shows a dimension of early Christianity that is entirely centered on the death of Jesus as the saving act. Also, the sermon shows us more clearly than any other NT writing the extent to which the interpretation of the OT played a role in the development of early Christian thought.

Theology of Hebrews:

- Christ is seen as the new Word of God, the communication of God to humanity in a new language that is personal. It is a word spoken in the life and death of a human being who is also God's Son.

- Christ functions as the unique, eternal high priest whose self-sacrifice inaugurates a new Covenant, and provides a new and open access to God.

- Christ's own insight into the heavenly world of God is the model of faith that Christians need to persevere in their hope.

(Notes taken from: *The Collegeville Bible Commentary, Vol.8.* Collegeville, MN: The Liturgical Press, 1983; *The New Jerome Bible Handbook*. Collegeville, MN: The Liturgical Press, 1993).

- <u>Small Group Work</u>

1.   Read Heb 1:1-5. What does it say about Jesus Christ?

2.   Read Heb 2:1-18. What is the importance of Jesus' humanity?

3.   Read Heb 7:1-28. What is the meaning of Christ's priesthood?

4.   Read Heb 8. What can you learn about the Old and the New Covenants?

5.   Read Heb 11:1-12:2. What does it say about faith and the cloud of witnesses? How can these ideas help us today?

● <u>Other Letters of Special Significance</u>

▪ The first Letter of Paul to the Thessalonians

The second coming is at hand!

1 Thessalonians is the earliest writing in the New Testament and, therefore, the oldest extant document of Christianity. In the past, the Letter has been interpreted in the light of the Book of Acts, but considering that Acts was written 30-35 years later and after Paul's death, it has become clear that 1 Thess should not be read in the light of Acts but just the opposite.

Thessalonica was an important port city in northern Greece founded about 316 B.C.E. Conquered by the Romans in 168, it became the capital of the Roman province of Macedonia after 146. Paul, Silvanus, and Timothy arrived in Thessalonica in 50 C.E., in the course of Mission II. When Paul wrote 1 Thess two or three years later, his letter-writing style was not yet fixed. He was in the process of breaking some literary conventions of his time and forging a new means of communication, the Christian Letter.

The Letters to the Thessalonians do not have the doctrinal importance of the four Great Letters or the Captivity Letters. Nevertheless, since they are the earliest NT writings, they provide us with a vivid picture of a young and fervent Christian community 20 years after the ascension.

In 1 Thess, the primary saving event is seen as the coming of the Lord at the end time (*parousia*). The Thessalonians expected that event to occur in their lifetime. This eschatological teaching was the source of courage and patience in the face of tribulation.

As usual, Paul's success with the Jews was minimal. After

three Sabbaths in the synagogue, he centered his activity among the Greeks. Many Gentiles and important women were converted. Paul gently encouraged this congregation to have confidence as the day of the Lord approaches and tells them to go about their everyday lives in a calm, responsible, and loving manner.

• The Letter of Paul to the Galatians

Paul writes to the "churches of Galatia" (1:2). Scholars do not agree upon the specific identity of the Galatians. Today, most believe that Paul wrote the letter to the predominantly Gentile communities in North Galatia (Turkey). It has been suggested that the letter was written between 54-55 C.E. for converts to Christianity from paganism (see Gal 4:8; 5:2-3; 6:12-13).

Shortly after Paul converted them, Judaizing Christians came along and argued that in order to be a good Christian one had first to be a good Jew by being circumcised and by observing other prescriptions of the Torah. These seem to have been Christians of some exaggerated or strict Jewish background, which set them apart from the group of moderate Jewish Christians represented by Apostles such as Peter, Paul, and even James. Paul was accused of watering down the requirements of the Gospel for the sake of the Gentiles.

Paul learned of the fascination of the Galatians for these new demands of the Judaizers and of the confusion this caused in the Galatian communities. This prompted him to send a strong and polemic letter, warning the churches against this "different gospel," defending his position as an Apostle, stressing the Christian's new-found freedom *vis-a-vis* the Law, and insisting that his gospel was the only correct view of Christianity. Although he calls the Galatians "senseless" (3:1), he still finds room in his heart for "my children" (4:19) and "brothers" (4:12; 5:11).

- <u>Small Group Work</u>

1. Read Paul's First Letter to the Thessalonians.

    a) What does Paul tell us about himself and his relationship to the people in 1 Thess 2:7?

    b) This letter suggests that actions are the only appropriate expression of faith (1 Thess 1:3). What does it mean for the community of Thessalonica? What concrete application does it have for today's Christian?

    c) If Paul were to write today about the expectation of the return of Christ, what would he say to modern readers in this regard?

2. Read Galatians 2. What was the Council of Jerusalem?

3. Read Galatians 4:8-19. Why was Paul so upset?

4. Read Galatians 5:1-6:10.

    a) How is Paul exhorting the community to remain free?

    b) What does he say about the proper use of freedom?

    c) How does he describe the fruits of the Spirit which is love (agápe), together with nine other qualities that should characterize a believer's relationship with other believers (5:22-23)?

● <u>The Pastoral Letters: First and Second Timothy, Titus</u>

These letters are called "pastoral" because they are addressed to pastors of Christian communities and because they deal with church life and practice. Although most scholars agree that Paul did not actually composed these letters, they were intended by their genuine author to be taken as Pauline statements, in accord with Pauline traditions.

The pastoral letters focus on Christian churches in the Aegean area and especially in Asia Minor. This has led most scholars to suppose that they originated somewhere in this region, perhaps in Ephesus. The Date proposed for them is before or around 100 C.E.

Timothy and Titus were two of Paul's closest companions. According to Acts 16:1-3 Timothy, who was born of mixed Jewish and Pagan parents, had become a Christian and began to follow Paul. (See 1 Thess 3:2, 6; 1 Cor 4:17; 16:10-11; Phil 2:19-23; Rom 16:21; 2 Cor 1:1, etc.).

Titus, a Gentile convert, came with Paul to the Jerusalem conference c. 49 C.E., and Paul claimed that he had refused at that time to have him circumcised (Gal 2:1, 3-5). Titus later accomplished a delicate mission to Corinth to patch up relations between Paul and that community (2 Cor 12:18; 2:13; 7:6-7, 13-16) and then served there as Paul's delegate for the gathering of the Jerusalem collection (2 Cor 8:6, 16-24).

What the author of the pastoral letters did intend was to urge church leaders to value and maintain order. He envisioned Christianity as a worldwide and fully unified movement that fulfilled the deepest aspirations of contemporary Roman culture for harmony in the family and in society. The author viewed Pauline Christianity as the only true philosophy or way of life.

Some of the "false teachings" mentioned in the letters could refer to a confused type of Jewish Christianity. Also they point to a very negative view of the physical world that opposed marriage and urged strict abstinence from food.

- <u>Small Group Work</u>

1. Read 1 Tim 1:3-7. What is the author's concern?

2. Read 1 Tim 4. What does it teach us about God's Creation?

3. Read 2 Tim 2. What can we learn from it?

4. Read Titus 1:5-9. What are the qualifications of church leaders according to this letter?

Is it true that James and Paul disagreed
about the way they interpreted salvation?
Did Paul believe in "faith alone"
and James in "works alone"?

• The Letter of James

The author is not likely one of the two members of the Twelve named James (see Matthew 10:2-3; Mark 3:17-18; Luke 6:14-15), for he is not identified as an Apostle but only as "slave of God and of the Lord Jesus Christ" (James 1:1) This designation probably refers to the third New Testament character named James, a relative of Jesus who is usually called "brother of the Lord" (see Matthew 13:55; Mark 6:3). He was the leader of the Jewish Christian community in Jerusalem whom Paul acknowledged as one of the "pillars" (Gal 2:9). In Acts he appears as the authorized spokesman for the Jewish Christian position in the early Church (Acts 12:17; 15:13-21).

Others, however, believe it more likely that James is a pseudonymous work of a later period. In addition to its Greek style, they observe further that: (a) the prestige that the writer is assumed to enjoy points to the later legendary reputation of James; (b) the discussion of the importance of good works seems to presuppose a debate subsequent to that in Paul's own day; (c) the author does not rely upon prescriptions of the Mosaic Law, as we would expect from the historical James; (d) the letter contains no allusions to James' own history and to his relationship with Jesus or to the early Christian community of Jerusalem. For these reasons, many recent interpreters assign James to the period 90-100.

Numerous passages in James treat subjects that also appear in the synoptic sayings of Jesus, especially in Matthew's Sermon on the Mount. James represents a type of early

Christianity that emphasized sound teaching and responsible moral behavior. Ethical norms are derived not primarily from Christology, as in Paul, but from a concept of salvation that involves conversion, baptism, forgiveness of sin, and expectation of judgment (James 1:17; 4:12).

The first conflict between the messages of Paul and James is described in the book of Acts. Acts 15 is the story of the Council at Jerusalem, where the leadership decided that Gentiles were not required to be circumcised in order to become Christians. Circumcision was closely linked to following Jewish Law. The strict view was that *it was necessary for them to be circumcised and ordered to keep the Law of Moses* –Acts 15:5. Paul responded with the evidence of the wonders done among Gentiles, people who are not circumcised, and are not keeping the Law. Paul's point was that only faith in Jesus Christ is necessary for salvation. It is James who proposed the compromise—that Gentiles should abstain from food offered to idols, strangled foods, and from blood, and from fornication.

Paul's commitment to grace and James' support of the Law are both the convictions of first century Jewish-Christians with roots in Palestinian Judaism.

It is a mistake to presume that James is not concerned with faith. Despite our general understanding that the letter is about works, James writes about faith from beginning to end. "Deeds do not replace faith, they complete it." The letter uses the word *faith* 16 times, although not so much to develop a theology, as to consider the practical implications of a life of faith. Yet it is clear that James wants us to know that the implication of faith IS *works*.

James is not denying Paul's contention that we are *justified by faith*, but he is opposed to the idea that we are justified by faith *alone. So faith by itself, if it has no works, is dead* –James 2:17. It is not that faith is unimportant, but rather that faith without works is not faith at all. James' concern is that faith and works must be unified, his goal is completeness and integrity. It is our actions at living out the Law that reveals our faith.

Certainly Paul and James would agree that we cannot say to a person without food: *"Go in peace; keep warm and eat your fill,"* unless we are willing to supply their bodily needs. For indeed, *"What is the good of that?"* (James 2:16).

• <u>Small Group Work</u>

In your own words, explain the connection between faith and good works in the plan of salvation.

*Is it true that the Book of Revelation
discloses the future and the things to come?
Are the crises in our world today predicted in this Book?*

• The Apocalypse: The Book of Revelation

Title: Latin *re-velare*, Greek *apo-kaluptein* = to remove the veil which hides the end of time, to unveil the end of history.

Date: Probably written about 95-100, but the author pretends that he is writing about 60. The Book of Revelation understands that the Emperor Domitian (81-96) is in fact the reincarnation of Nero and is now persecuting the Christians in Asia Minor. Jews and Christians were violently persecuted because they would not pay the exorbitant taxes imposed upon them nor would they acclaim the Emperor as Lord. The persecution and the time of the writing of Revelation occurred in the mid-90's.

Audience: The Book is addressed to the Christians of Asia Minor, modern day Turkey.

Purpose: Mainly to give Christians **hope in the face of persecution.**

Literary Character: The Book has been influenced by three literary forms:

a) Apocalyptic   *b) prophetic*   *c) epistolary*

Prophecy which was strong during the monarchy, declined during the Babylonian exile, and was all but dead by the year 300 B.C.E. The prophetic hope of God's final intervention to destroy evil and establish his kingdom began to fade as Babylonian, Persian, Greek and Roman domination followed one another. Many turned to a political hope, but others kept to the prophetic dream — from this the apocalyptic literary form developed. It recalled past victories by placing them in a dramatic future tense, as if they were foretold long before it happened. This type of writing flourished during periods of persecution and upheaval when the Jews or the Christians were suffering for their faith.

Apocalyptic literature employs all kinds of imagery and symbolism which appeal to the imagination of the readers. It is the product of an indestructible Jewish hope in the "age to come," the "Day of the Lord." In the Bible there are two works written in this apocalyptic style: Daniel and Revelation. Daniel was written during the persecution of the Syrians c.165 B.C.E. Revelation was written during the persecution of the Roman Emperor Domitian in the mid-90's C.E.

Both works had as their object to impress upon the faithful Jews *(Daniel)* and the faithful Christians *(Revelation)* that the Lord would champion his people in the face of persecution, that the people of God would be victorious in the long run. Therefore, they have every reason for hope. Their enemies will be punished by God.

• The Apocalypse and its Symbols

(Sources: *The Jerome Biblical Commentary; The Apocalypse* by Rev. Patrick J. Sena, C. PP.S.; *How to Read the New Testament* by Etienne Charpentier; *The Book of Revelation* by Pheme Perkins).

Symbols, so cherished by Apocalyptic writers, are in evidence everywhere; their presence is explicitly signaled (1:20), and their meaning is sometimes explained (5:6, 8; 13:18; 17:9-18).

Most of the symbols of the Ap are borrowed from the prophetic tradition continued by the Apocalyptic. e.g.:

A woman represents a people (12:1ff.) Or a city (17:1ff.)

Horns speak of power (5:6; 12:3), in particular, dynastic power (13:1; 17:3ff.)

Eyes, knowledge (1:14; 2:18; 4:6; 5:6)

Wings, mobility (4:8; 12:14)

Trumpets transmit a superhuman, divine voice (1:10; 8:2ff.)

A Sharp Sword indicates the Word of God, which judges and punishes (1:16; 2:12, 16; 19:15, 21)

White robes signify the world of glory (6:11; 7:9,13ff.; 22:14)

Palms are the sign of triumph (7:9)

Crowns, of dominion and kingship (2:10; 3:11; 4:10; 6:2; 12:1; 14:14)

The Sea is an evil element, source of insecurity and death (13:1; 21:1)

White indicates the joy of victory (1:14; 2:17; 3:4ff., 18; 4:4; 6:11; 7:9,13; 19:11,14)

Read, violence or war

Purple, luxury and kingship (17:4; 18:12,16)

Black, death (6:5, 12)

Numbers. Among the ancients, **numbers** held a very important place. Before the invention of the Arabic numerals, letters were used for numbers. In the Book of Revelation symbolic numbers acquire a considerable importance and some occur over and over again. e.g.:

7 **Seven** (54 times) signifies fullness, perfection. Seven beatitudes 1:3; 14:13; 16:15; 19:9; 20:6; 22:7; 22:14;
Seven attributes of the Lamb 5:12;
Seven blessings in heaven 7:15-17

12 **Twelve** (23 times), being a multiple of 3x4, also shares in the perfection of 7. It recalls the 12 tribes of Israel and indicates that the people of God has reached its eschatological perfection.

4 **Four** (16 times) symbolizes the universality of the visible world (e.g. the four corners of the earth).

6 **Six** is less than perfect or evil (13:18).

0   **1000 and all numbers with zeroes** indicate an unlimited number, an immeasurable quantity. Thus, 12,000 signifies a perfect unlimited number, the same can be said for 144,000 (7:4).

- The Beast: Rev 13:18

"A certain wisdom is needed here; with a little ingenuity anyone can calculate the number of the beast, for it is a number that stands for a certain man. The man's number is six hundred and sixty-six." (13:18)

13:1-10: The beast from the sea. The beasts (one from the sea and one from the earth) symbolize the Antichrist and false prophet of the end time in Jewish Apocalyptic visions. At the same time they are the final embodiment of imperial power opposed to the rule of God. The sea indicates that the beast in question embodies the watery chaos monster of ancient Near Eastern mythology, the primordial source of all evil.

The author identifies the beast for his audience by reminding them of a piece of esoteric numerology that would apparently have been well known to Christians in such circumstances: **the number of the Beast is 666. This number is not a prediction of the future... this code is one which the author and his audience share.**

Ancient Hebrew/Aramaic did not contain numbers separate from their letters. Like the Romans who used Roman numerals (letters for numbers), so the people of the Bible used their letters as numerals. The first Roman Emperor to persecute the Christians was the Emperor Nero (54-68 C.E.). In the Hebrew/Aramaic Alphabet the expression "Nero Caesar" in Hebrew would be written in transliteration as follows:

N-50	R-200	W-6	N-50	Q-100	S-60	R-200
Neron						**Caesar**

In Hebrew and Greek, "Nero" is spelled "Neron" with a final "n." This is not the case in Latin. It is easily seen that someone transliterating from Latin and not realizing that the Hebrew rendition of the Emperor's name contained a final "n," would have omitted the final "n." N is the number 50. For this reason some manuscripts read 616 instead of 666. The ancients readily understood that our author was indicating Nero Caesar with the number 666.

(Sources: *The Book of Revelation* by Pheme Perkings, and *The Apocalypse* by Rev. Patrick J. Sena, C.PP.S.)

Why are so many people saying that this book predicts the END? There are even movies with this theme!

- <u>Interpreting the Apocalypse</u>

The Apocalypse should not be understood as a puzzle which has remained hidden for over two thousand years. Such an approach would deny the fact that all Scripture has a meaning for the people of every age. Throughout history there have been four basic approaches to understanding the Book:

- The Book treats of the end times and the final days.
- The Book treats of a projection of all history of every age leading to the final day of the second coming.
- The Book has universal spiritual principles that have meaning for every age.
- The Book was written for a specific time and a specific occasion: that of the reign of the Emperor Domitian, and it also has meaning for us today.

- <u>Other confusing topics:</u>

- **A thousand-year reign (Rev 20:4-6).** This section has combined several apocalyptic themes. It draws from a section in Ezekiel 37-43 which contains end-time images of salvation: the Messiah rules; Gog and Magog are defeated; the new Jerusalem is described. Revelation pictures a rule by the Messiah prior to the defeat of Gog and Magog. This section in Rev also has mixed traditions about the resurrection which reflect the different images of the first century.

  To understand the concept of the millennium we need to place it within the context of the persecution of the Christians by the Emperor Domitian. Those who lost their lives under the Emperor have been reigning with Christ. The number 1000 can signify a limitless reign with the Lord.

- **Dispensationalism** is a system for interpreting the Bible founded by John Nelson Darby (1800-1882). Believers in **Dispensationalism** look forward to an actual 1000 year reign. Dispensationalism is not in accord with mainstream Christian thought.

- **The Rapture.** Originated in the Latin Bible translation of 400 C.E. In Latin the word *rapio* means "to seize or snatch." It is found in 2 Cor 12:4 and in 1 Thes 4:17. The language was used to describe the arrival of the Emperor or some far-eastern important person. In Apocalyptic language it is used to describe a very wondrous event.

  The doctrine of the "Rapture" "rose about 150 years ago among some Protestants in Britain and later spread to the United States through popular revival preachers. Its proponents think that Jesus will return not once but twice. His first will be a "secret" coming to "snatch" true believers from the world and then the Old Testament prophecies against Israel will be fulfilled. Then it will follow a time of great tribulation and suffering, with natural catastrophes and the persecution of the antichrist. Then again Christ will come to finally establish his reign. Often proponents of this theory have an anti-Catholic agenda.

Catholics maintain that the future is in God's hands and will unfold according to his plan. The earthly Jesus trusted God's plan about the future (see Mark 13:32) and so do we!

- Small Group Work

1.   Read Revelation 2-3 (The Seven Letters).

These letters written to Christian churches of Asia Minor, follow a very strict literary pattern. They have the same introduction and conclusion, with only some variations in details. The body of each letter is also constructed according to the same form. In each letter, the author articulates what he thinks is the problem of the churches and why such difficulty has befallen the society.

Pay attention to the section of each letter which begins, "But I have this against you…"

   • What does the author think is wrong with Christianity in his day?

- Does this problem have any counterpart in our modern day?

Ephesus (2:1-7)

Smyrna (2:8-11)

Pergamum (2:12-17)

Thyatira (2:18-29)

Sardis (3:1-6)

Philadelphia (3:7-13)

Laodicia (3:14-22)

2. Read Revelation 1:4. Who is the "One who is who was and who is to come"?

3. Read Rev 20:11-15. What is the role of the One who was sitting on the large white throne?

4.   Read Rev 21:1 - 22:5.
      What imagery is used to describe the new Jerusalem?
      Why is this new Jerusalem so special?

5.   In what ways might this vision of the new Jerusalem
      be a source of hope for an oppressed people? Do we
      have anything comparable in our culture today?

6.   What is the "menu" for the banquet at the end time
      (19:17-18)? As a symbolic myth for an oppressed peo-
      ple, what might the banquet represent?

7.   What is the symbolic meaning of the thousand year
      period of the binding of Satan (20:1-10)? To what event
      is the author referring when he speaks of the time in
      which Satan will be released from prison?

Epilogue

The 1st Letter of John tells us that, "God is Love" (4:16). This definition of the nature of God summarizes what the Bible means to me. Every book of the Bible, with its own literary style and the human and social limitations of the sacred writers, tries to reveal to us the awesome and unconditional love of God.

The Bible is not only filled with fascinating events and extraordinary people; it also contains the story of God's radical love for Creation.

I hope that these pages have helped you to better understand the richness and depth of the Scriptures. My wish is that you may come to know the Word made flesh, the God Incarnate, the God with us! If this book has facilitated in any way a deeper encounter with the living and loving God, I am grateful. Then, in these turbulent times, you and I will come to understand that "there is no fear in love, but perfect love casts out fear." (1 John 4:18)

In the Bibliography, I recommend basic as well as more advanced books that have been of assistance to me in this wonderful adventure with the Word of God.

I conclude with the blessing that Yahweh gave to Moses for the people of Israel:

> "The Lord bless you and keep you!
> The Lord let his face shine upon you,
> and be gracious to you!
> The Lord look upon you kindly
> and give you peace!"

Numbers 6:24-26

BIBLIOGRAPHY

Commentaries

Bergant, C.S.A., Dianne, ed. *The Collegeville Bible Commentary. Old Testament.* Collegeville: The Liturgical Press, 1992.

Brown, S.S., Raymond E., Fitzmeyer, S.J., Joseph A., Murphy, O.Carm., Roland E. *The New Jerome Biblical Commentary,* New Jersey: Prentice Hall, 1990.

The New Jerome Bible Handbook. Collegeville: The Liturgical Press, 1993.

Hiesberger, Jean Marie, ed. *The Catholic Bible. Personal Study Edition.* New York: Oxford University Press, 1995.

Karris, O.F.M., Robert J., ed. *The Collegeville Bible Commentary. New Testament.* Collegeville: The Liturgical Press, 1992.

Stuhlmueller, C.P., Carroll, ed. *The Collegeville Pastoral Dictionary of Biblical Theology.* Collegeville: The Liturgical Press, 1996.

Church Documents

Encyclical Divino Afflante Spiritu, Pope Pius XII, September 30, 1943.

Dogmatic Constitution on Divine Revelation: Dei Verbum. Vatican II Documents. Solemnly promulgated by his holiness Pope Paul VI on November 18, 1965.

Pastoral Statement for Catholics on Biblical Fundamentalism.

National Conference of Catholic Bishops Ad-hoc Committee on Biblical Fundamentalism. Washington, D.C., March 26, 1987.

The Interpretation of the Bible in the Church. Pontifical Biblical Commission. Libreria Editrice Vaticana. November, 1993. Reprinted in English, Origins, VOL.23: NO.29, January 6, 1994.

Books

Boadt, Lawrence. *Reading the Old Testament.* New York: Paulist Press, 1984.

Bright, John. *A History of Israel.* Philadelphia: Westminster Press, 1981.

Brown, S.S., Raymond E. *An Introduction to the New Testament.* New York: Doubleday, 1997.

_____. *An Introduction to New Testament Christology.* New York: Paulist Press, 1994.

_____. *Antioch & Rome.* New York: Paulist Press, 1983.

_____. *The Community of the Beloved Disciple.* New York: Paulist Press, 1979.

_____. *The Churches the Apostles Left Behind.* New York: Paulist Press, 1984.

Brueggemann, Walter. *Texts That Linger, Words That Explode.* Minneapolis: Fortress Press, 2000.

Charpentier, Etienne. *How to Read the Old Testament.* New York: Crossroad, 1990.

_____. *How to Read the New Testament*. New York: Crossroad, 1990.

Ellis, Peter. "The Historicity of the Gospels," in *Matthew: His Mind and His Message*. Collegeville: The Liturgical Press, 1974.

Flanagan, OSM, Neal M. *Mark, Matthew, Luke: A Guide to the Gospel Parallels*. Collegeville: The Liturgical Press, 1978.

Newsome, Jr., James D. *The Hebrew Prophets*. Atlanta: John Knox Press, 1984.

Nickle, Keith F. *The Synoptic Gospels*, Atlanta: SCM Press Ltd., 1981.

Perkins, Pheme. *The Book of Revelation*. Collegeville: The Liturgical Press, 1983.

Schneiders, Sandra M. *Written That You May Believe*. New York: The Crossroad Publishing Co., 1999.

Schüssler Fiorenza, Elisabeth. *But She said: Feminist Practices of Biblical Interpretation*. Boston: Beacon, 1992.

Sena, C.PP.S., Patrick. *The Apocalypse*. New York: Alba House, 1983.